Autistic
Songs

Autistic Songs

Alan Griswold

iUniverse, Inc.
Bloomington

Autistic Songs

iUniverse books may be ordered through booksellers or by contacting:

iUniverse
1663 Liberty Drive
Bloomington, IN 47403
www.iuniverse.com
1-800-Authors (1-800-288-4677)

ISBN: 978-1-4502-9994-7 (pbk)
ISBN: 978-1-4502-9995-4 (ebk)

Printed in the United States of America

iUniverse rev. date: 3/10/2011

Contents

Preface

Autism has now acquired many enemies, and nearly all have gathered under the protective banner of conventional wisdom. Advocacy groups, cognitive scientists, lawmakers, geneticists, academicians—nearly everywhere one turns, one can find yet another self-assured group relying upon conventional wisdom to ascribe defective characteristics to autistic individuals, and to opine on how autism serves as the obvious counterexample to the traits which define humanity. To cite just one prominent instance, we have Steven Pinker—the famed linguist, cognitive scientist and author of five best-selling books on the nature of language and thought—who in *The Blank Slate* (Pinker 2002) quickly dismisses autistic individuals with all the pithiness we have come to expect from Steven Pinker: "Together with robots and chimpanzees, people with autism remind us that cultural learning is possible only because neurologically normal people have innate equipment to accomplish it." When it comes to autism (and cultural learning, for that matter), Steven Pinker is no stranger to conventional wisdom.

The only class of people I have found who do not routinely embrace autism's conventional wisdom are autistic individuals themselves. Sounding distinctly *unlike* robots and chimpanzees, autistic individuals will often describe their experiences with a wide range of ability, thought and emotion, descriptions that can be brutally honest about the challenges autistic individuals must face, while at the same time being abundantly enthusiastic about the many possibilities autism has to offer.

Unconventional possibilities.

Autism is a condition that, perhaps more than anything else, embraces the unconventional. Autism transforms the unconventional into an entire mode of being. And lest we dismiss that mode of being too quickly, and with too much pithiness, we should note how highly contagious unconventionality has become. For those conventional thinkers who have convinced themselves autism's strangeness and abnormality serve as the obvious contrast to the traits which define humanity, might I suggest that, when it comes to humanity, they take a wider look around. Man as a species may be many things upon this planet, but the one thing man most assuredly is not, is conventional.

I have heard the perfect reply being made to Steven Pinker's particular brand of ignorance. I have it heard it being made by an autistic individual. Michelle Dawson is a woman without the fame, credentials or glib manner of a Steven Pinker, but she is a woman who has nonetheless drawn deeply upon her autistic characteristics to reveal invaluable insights into the nature of autistic intelligence and who has become one of the more influential—if albeit unconventional—researchers in the autism field. Michelle Dawson often encapsulates her hard-earned knowledge with a catchphrase I find more pithy and certainly far more accurate than anything that has ever passed Steven Pinker's lips: "Autistics deserve better."

This book is the avowed enemy of conventional wisdom, and in its pages you will hear that autistics do indeed deserve better. Therefore, let us begin to sing their praise.

Autistic Songs

The motto here is always: Take a *wider* look around.

Ludwig Wittgenstein

Intelligence

The First Step Is the One That Altogether Escapes Notice

It must have seemed an obvious choice—not even much of a choice really—to take autism as the sign of something gone horribly wrong. There was the example of schizophrenia helping to lay the groundwork, and now the unveiling of all these disconnected children, so clearly different and apparently destroyed.

We have been exploring autism's geography for more than sixty years now and have visited a veritable travel tour's delight of promised lands: Refrigerator Mother Mountain, Blind Mind Alley, Genome Dome, and the Swamp of a Thousand Toxins. Having journeyed for so long and having charted a course so wide, surely our much scribbled-upon map must now be showing great progress.

Except, of course, that first step was in the wrong direction.

Historical IQ

What would happen if we gave a modern IQ test to one of the ancients—a Mesopotamian, an Egyptian, the average Athenian citizen (Meletus, for instance)? How many block designs might we expect before sundown? How much arithmetic without mistake? Similarities? Picture completion?

When we measure intelligence, what capacities are we already assuming, and where and when did these capacities originate? Are we sure we want to keep looking in the frontal, parietal and occipital lobes?

The Flynn effect should not surprise us. After all, it was not that long ago the average human did not possess enough intelligence to *take* an IQ test, let alone analyze its calendar-sensitive results.

Tautology

Today's word is *tautology*.

> tau·tol·o·gy, noun:
> 1. a needless repetition of an idea in different words or phrases;
> 2. a representation of anything as the cause, condition, or consequence of itself.

In its everyday guise, a tautology can often be mistaken as a significant statement—it usually takes some thought and a little insight to recognize tautological statements as devoid of any substance. A simple example would be: "I've researched the matter thoroughly and have come to the conclusion that without exception bachelors are not married. What's more, everyone agrees with me." This assertion has been gussied up to *sound* significant, but of course a moment's consideration exposes the statement as little more than an empty fidgeting with an agreed-upon definition.

But not all tautologies are so easily unmasked:

A: "Autism is a terrible disorder, a horrible disease."

B: "But my child has autism and she doesn't seem particularly troubled by it. True, she has some language difficulties she's working through, and she's not particularly interested in what the other kids do and say. But she's smart, sweet, funny, curious—full of delight. She's going to be just fine."

A: "Then your child does not have autism. She may be *recovering* from autism, or she may have some mild variation that is not autism itself. But people with autism, without exception, are severely affected by the condition. That's what autism is—a terrible disorder, a horrible disease."

If we are going to systematically exclude from the category of autism all individuals who are doing well, then statements about autism being a disorder or a disease lose all their significance—they become vacuous, tautological. This practice goes a long ways towards explaining why we have gained so little insight regarding autism over the last sixty years, because we are never going to understand a condition in which we insist on seeing only those individuals who are troubled, while willfully ignoring all those who are propelled.

Autistics Think Differently Than Non-Autistics—Dramatically So

The Level and Nature of Autistic Intelligence (Dawson et al. 2007) is a simple report—so simple its gist can be gleaned from just one of its pictures, that of Figure 3. But oh my, what a shattering image that is! Think of Alzheimer's versus controls. Think of mercury poisoning versus controls. Can we not surmise the same garden-variety distribution, only drifted farther down the diagonal? Autistics shock us not only with their northwesterly cluster—stunning enough as that is—but also in their clinging to the edges of the graph, like prisoners longing to escape the yard.

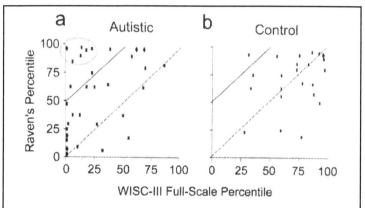

Fig. 3. Relation between Full Scale IQ on the Wechsler Intelligence Scale for Children–Third Edition (WISC-III) and Raven's Progressive Matrices scores in (a) autistic children and (b) control children. Data points to the left of the dashed diagonal lines represent subjects whose Raven's Matrices scores were greater than their WISC-III scores; data points to the left of the solid diagonal lines represent subjects whose Raven's Matrices scores were 50 percentile points greater than their WISC-III scores. In (a), a circle surrounds the data points for 7 autistic children whose Raven's Matrices scores exceeded their WISC-III scores by more than 70 percentile points. Diamonds represent identical data points from 2 subjects.

Raven's Progressive Matrices

The Raven's Progressive Matrices intelligence test (RPM) is a pure space and time test. Note how the two-dimensional patterns are not random, but are designed to highlight various forms of geometrical, symmetrical and conceptual structure—the fundamental basis for our notion of space. And note how the image-to-image changes also are not random, but are designed to capture regular patterns of events—the fundamental basis for our notion of time.

Because RPM measures ability to apprehend spatial and temporal pattern, it should not surprise us that autistic individuals perform comparatively well on this test. These results have less to do with the fact that the test is non-verbal than with the fact the test captures the essence of the autistic individual's natural cognitive domain.

Beethoven

What a strange scherzo to hear Beethoven revered as one of the old masters, a fatherly icon of classical music. What amusing irony to see him accepted by the appropriate crowd.

Listen to that diabolical music! An affront to all classical sentiment, much of it sounding like a meltdown set to notes.

Genius—respectable only in retrospect.

Music and Raven's Progressive Matrices

The Raven's Progressive Matrices intelligence test may be the nearest thing humans have to a pure space and time test. The Raven's spatial/temporal problem domain, natural to autistic perception and cognition, helps explain why autistic individuals perform so differentially well on that particular test.

Yet there is at least one other human endeavor that shares a similar structure to the Raven's test—namely music. The roles played by rhythm, melody and harmony are quite analogous to the roles played by time, space and conceptual pattern in Raven's, and the well-documented affinity and natural ability many autistic individuals evince for music is further suggestive of an underlying connection.

Time, space, geometry, arithmetic, logic, melody, harmony, rhythm, games, rules, syntax—these concepts run along the contours and fault lines of autistic cognition. Understanding their inter-connectedness helps to highlight the nature of autistic perception and helps to characterize autistic contribution to human endeavor. Music and the Raven's intelligence test are not random gewgaws from the stream of life—their prominence derives from their correlation to the forces driving the human species forward.

Intelligence, Genius, and Autism

Professor James Flynn has incorporated an interesting sidebar into his book *What Is Intelligence?* (Flynn 2007). In it he lists his seven choices for Western civilization's greatest minds: Pythagoras, Plato, Aristotle, Archimedes, Newton, Gauss, and Einstein. The exact intent of the term "greatest minds" is left somewhat unclear—in fact, it sounds like deliberate fudging to me—but elsewhere in the sidebar discussion Professor Flynn suggests it is *intelligence* that is being discussed; these are Professor Flynn's choices for history's most *intelligent* men.

But of course if it is intelligence that is being discussed, then Professor Flynn's list must be complete and utter nonsense. It is nonsense, ironically enough, precisely because of the Flynn effect, for as a direct corollary of that discovery, I should find I can walk onto almost any street at this very moment and at random choose seven individuals who could put Professor Flynn's list to shame by any standard measure of human intelligence. That is what the Flynn effect means—or at least that is what it means if we, and Professor Flynn, are going to take it seriously.

Yet, truth be told, I actually have no argument with the selections on Professor Flynn's list; to me, the list seems extraordinarily well chosen. Admittedly, I can think of other individuals also worthy of inclusion, but what remains compelling about Professor Flynn's list is that he has attempted to capture a rare, valuable and immensely powerful human characteristic, and each one of his selections serves as an ideal example of that very characteristic. The problem I have is not with the individuals Professor Flynn has chosen, the problem I have is with the *name* he has given to his list's defining characteristic; for it would seem Professor Flynn is confusing two very different concepts—he is confusing intelligence and genius. The seven men on Professor Flynn's list are not examples of great intelligence, they are instead examples of profound genius. And even more telling, the seven men on Professor Flynn's list are examples also of the transformational power of autism.

When it comes to understanding the true nature of intelligence I am certain I must live in a very dark age, the age of brain science ascendancy. Hundreds of research teams, maybe even thousands by now, have so convinced themselves that intelligence must originate from inside our skulls, have so convinced themselves that only within networks of cranial neurons can be found the secrets to humanity's growing mental capacity, that all have managed to overlook completely the far more plausible alternative—the one existing right before our very eyes.

Having no access myself to expensive pieces of neuroimaging equipment, having never secured the necessary funding for series of nuanced, split-second psychiatric experiments, I will begin instead by asking only a simple question: how intelligent was the human species approximately fifty thousand years ago? At around 50,000 B.C., how well would the average man have scored on any intelligence test?

If by intelligence we mean that set of skills that translates into enhanced performance on the modern forms of Stanford-Binet, Wechsler, Raven's, and all the other intelligence scales—skills that correlate to better outcomes in academics and career and that lead on average to more favorable circumstances within modern society—then it must be abundantly clear that fifty thousand years ago the average man possessed hardly any intelligence at all. Fifty thousand years ago, what humans possessed were the same skills as all the other animals possessed—skills appropriate and essential for survival and procreation, but skills that would not have been (and still would not be today) of much use on any intelligence test, because in point of fact, those are precisely the skills that get excluded from measure.

Look at the *content* of any intelligence test—language, arithmetic, patterns, designs. What we measure with the aid of those IQ booklets are not the abilities we inherited from out our animal past, but instead their exact counterpart; we measure only those skills the species has been adding throughout all its history since. In some sense, an intelligence test measures the *modernness* of an individual; an intelligence test measures an individual's ability to appropriate for himself the same set of skills the species has been appropriating as a whole—skills that do not find their origin in our biological nature, but instead owe their existence to the strange, brewing mixture of *non*-biological pattern, structure and form that has been rapidly taking shape all around us.

Rather than focusing on the *brain* of modern man, we should instead be examining more carefully his *surroundings*, a study that can be made quite stark by contrasting the surroundings of two such men, each placed at an extreme of modern man's timeline. The first man we will set down at the edge of the African savannah, near the beginning of man's great leap forward; and the other we can position on a street corner in midtown Manhattan, right here at the start of the twenty-first century.

For the man located near the edge of the savannah, at around the fiftieth millennium B.C., we see that he is living in a locale teeming with biological intrigue but utterly bereft of such things as symmetry, number and pattern. It is not that such things do not exist in nature— stems grow in straight lines, faces, moon and sun betray symmetry, there is binary structure in the exchange of day and night, and there is repetition in the celestial patterns—but compared to the man-made environments we live within today, the examples of precise form to be found in nature are surprisingly paltry. And besides, for the man living in such an environment, he would be under no compulsion, would experience no motivation, to notice any of these patterned features. For this man, just as with all the other animals, the only order of business is survival and procreation—survival and procreation alone. Even space and time cannot rise to the level of consciousness—for how exactly can space and time be measured—this man is locked entirely inside his biological immediacy. And what could we possibly expect in the way of language? With space, time, pattern, symmetry, abstraction and so much else removed from ken, what would this man have found occasion to talk about, what could he have possibly have needed to *say* that he could not instead immediately sense or do?

It would be no exaggeration to say that an intelligence test offered to such a man would be an exercise in futility. Never mind how we might uncover any set of skills for which he might register even one scintilla of a positive score, ask instead how we could *construct* such an exam, construct it so that he might comprehend the first step of what he was being requested to do. The first thing to understand about the Flynn effect is that it must have started near the dawn of modern man's history, because whatever humanity's average raw intelligence score might happen to be today, at the very beginning that score was undoubtedly zero.

When we leap ahead to the circumstances of the man standing on a New York street corner, we realize the contrast could hardly be greater, but that contrast cannot be found inside respective brains, not unless we believe fifty thousand years is an evolutionary eternity—the biology of the man on today's urban street is fundamentally no different than that of the man on the ancient savannah. No, the contrast is more clearly seen by simply taking a good look around. For the man living in today's surroundings, what we notice first is how much the natural world has been eclipsed from view—in midtown Manhattan there are only a few trees, a brief glimpse of sky, the occasional drop of rain to remind this man from where his ancestors have come. And even the many other humans who are bustling around him—the most abundant and natural connection to his animal past—they appear now as something strangely transformed, in haircuts, lipstick, perfume and shoes. Instead of the sights and sounds of nature, it is man-made construction that now thoroughly dominates his landscape, a construction guided by, and in turn reflecting, the manifold concepts of symmetry, pattern, repetition, structure and form. Each building towering above him is a cornucopia of symmetry. The streets play out in symphonies of grids and symbols and lines. Window abutting window puts forth a kind of arithmetic, and light after blinking light announces the rhythms of logic and computation. Finally there is the incessant rush of language: structured by the form it represents, language has now blossomed into something ubiquitous and multi-dimensional, from the thousands of whispered sidewalk conversations, to the countless billboards screaming what to buy, to the not-so-subtle exhortations of madly honking horns.

Looking at and listening to what this Manhattan man must experience in less than a moment's hesitation—the amount of structure, pattern and language literally cascading down around him—we might convince ourselves he must now be thoroughly overwhelmed, his senses must be completely overloaded (as would happen if we were to thrust this scene upon the savannah-dwelling man). But as a matter of fact we see that he is not overwhelmed at all, that having grown up in similar environments, having been trained from an early age to master all manner of structured nuance, he goes forth in such surroundings with the greatest of ease—hails a cab, reads a newspaper headline, calculates the number of minutes required to travel uptown—and if we were to bring him inside and place him before an IQ exam, he would not be in the slightest bit amazed. He would find its designs, arithmetic and patterns to be objects perfectly familiar; he would require only minimal instruction to be quickly up and running, soon to impress us with his abundantly positive score.

The present man's intelligence exceeds that of all who have gone before him because he lives in a far more intelligent setting, one increasingly suffused with pattern, structure, design. Today's man grows up in that environment, is trained to work ably within it, lives it, breathes it, appropriates it deeply within his being, and thereby goes forth smarter than all his forebears. The *form* of our human surroundings—*that* is the secret to our growing mental capacity. The fast-accumulating changes to our experienced world—these are the transformations keeping pace with the Flynn effect. The human environment, in its entirety—there can be found the source, and the sustenance, of our expanding human intelligence.

And to add one more timeline example, for the sake of completeness—and for the sake of clarifying Professor Flynn's list—let us consider the circumstances of one more individual, this one standing *between* the extremes of humanity's calendar. Let us consider the circumstances, the surroundings, the *intelligence* of an ancient Greek named Aristotle.

The achievements of the ancient Greeks continue to impress us because of how greatly they surpassed everything that had gone before. One might almost believe structure, pattern and form *began* in ancient Greece, so richly did that culture emblazon those concepts into its architecture, pottery, science, literature and lives. But as impressive as the artifacts of ancient Greece undoubtedly were, they pale in comparison to the richly etched and far more abundant creations of our modern times. The Acropolis buildings, for instance, sublime in 400 B.C., are little more than slab models next to the cathedrals, terminals and skyscrapers of today. The branches of Greek mathematics, marvels of logic in the ancient world, are in the twenty-first century only the lessons of elementary school. The ancient Greek language, that thing of beauty upon Homer's lips, in vocabulary and grammar stands far more crude and limited than even a simple email exchange. And finally we must consider the *pace* of ancient Greek life, never much faster than a horse's canter. At such a leisurely speed how could an Athenian citizen have experienced even a fraction of the informational structure we experience in less than a day, we who race madly from scene to scene in airplanes, buses and cars, and we who have landscapes rapidly thrust back upon us, on computers, televisions and phones?

The ancient Greek culture was unquestionably a burst of structure into our experienced world, and its members, absorbing that burst, would have displayed far more intelligence than the hunter-gatherers who had gone before (indeed the ancient Greeks would have been capable of *taking* an intelligence test, they could have differentiated themselves by means of their scores). But having been reared in surroundings much simpler, more crude than those of current times, having passed through life at a significantly slower pace, the ancient Greeks would have been overwhelmed by circumstances as hurried and complex as our own, would have been mostly befuddled by intelligence exams as sophisticated as ours. Aristotle would have been no different (neither would have Pythagoras, Plato or Archimedes). Intelligent relative to his peers, Aristotle would have been nonetheless no smarter than his circumstances could allow, and would have performed poorly and slowly on the equivalent of a modern intelligence exam. And it does no good to argue that I am somehow slighting Aristotle in this backwards-looking scenario, that I am somehow not allowing Aristotle's ample brain a fair enough chance. It does no good to argue that a man of his impressive cognitive ability, if he were to be raised in our modern world, if he were to be educated in one of our finer schools, if he were to be given the opportunity to experiment, to travel, would certainly score as brilliantly as any of us, nay even more so, on any modern intelligence exam—it does no good to make that argument at all, for when we stop to reflect about it, we realize that is precisely the point.

When we take the Flynn effect seriously, we see it cannot be just a twentieth-century phenomenon alone. It must have started well before the dawn of civilized history and has been shadowing human existence ever since. When we take the Flynn effect seriously, we understand it cannot be caused by better nutrition, selective breeding, greater education or a socially-driven multiplier effect—its roots run much deeper than that. And when we take the Flynn effect seriously, we learn something about the nature of intelligence; we learn intelligence is not a concept neuronally based, it does not exist primarily inside our heads.

Genius is the name often bestowed upon individuals such as the seven forming Professor Flynn's list, and although here the appellation is correct, the understanding is usually wrong. Conventional wisdom regards genius as evidence for a better brain, the marker of a smoother, faster-running neural machine; conventional wisdom regards genius as the equivalent of greater intelligence. But this conventional wisdom cannot possibly be accurate, for if it were, by the evidence of the Flynn effect alone, humans would be in possession of a different kind of brain today than they were in previous times, and here in the twenty-first century, genius would be blossoming as a commonplace trait. It is time to reconsider that conventional wisdom, time to regard genius with a different set of eyes; for genius is not a function of greater intelligence, genius is the *description* of how intelligence grows.

When we recognize intelligence to be the embodiment of non-biological form, structure and pattern to be found within our human surroundings, the question we must ask next is how do these tangible changes occur, why do they happen at all? The other animal species do not produce similar structural changes into their own environment, and neither did humans for a very long time. To take just the artifacts of the industrial revolution alone—engines, cars, factories, rockets, and so much more crowding the spaces all around us—we recognize, perhaps with some sense of surprise, that it was only a few hundred years ago these artifacts did not exist at all. So how did they come to be, why do we now find ourselves awash in their abundant intelligence? Perhaps it was started by an edict of nation, you say. Maybe a private corporation launched a project. Could it be that we owe a debt of gratitude to that modern front for genius, the academic research team?

Professor Flynn knows the answer: Professor Flynn recognizes how much our entire industrialized, mechanized world owes to the writings of just one man—owes to the work of Sir Isaac Newton.

Before Newton scribbled his three laws of motion into his notebook, before his descriptions of color and gravitation began to make the rounds, there was scarcely one whit of our now mechanically dominated world that had yet to grace the human eye, there was scarcely one hint of physical logic that had yet to nestle against human consciousness. But beginning in the summer of Newton's twenty-third year, a new door suddenly burst open, and through that door passed not only a world-altering material revolution, there passed also an avalanche of expanding human intelligence. The engines, cars, factories, rockets, and so much more crowding the spaces all around us—these artifacts exist not only as the *product* of Newton's equations and laws, they exist also as *reflections* of the knowledge contained within, thereby spreading their skill and logic literally all around. Abundantly familiar now with trains, satellites, gas pedals, bulldozers, prisms, telescopes, and all the rest, humans easily master the concepts of inertia, acceleration, differentiation, spectrum, force; for humans have been absorbing these concepts not by reading the pages of the *Principia Mathematica*, they have been absorbing these concepts by living amongst the *Principia's* many lingering effects.

Genius is the spark that sets the human world ablaze and helps re-create that world afresh.

An ironic feature of genius is that it does not of itself *add* the new intelligence into the human environment—Newton himself, for instance, produced not a single artifact of the industrial revolution. The broadcast, construction and accumulation of genius's vision—that is the work of all mankind, drawing heavily upon humanity's gregarious, imitative and socially selfish nature; and here can be found the reason genius is recognized almost always in hindsight, for it is only after its catalyzing effect has had sufficient opportunity to work that humanity gains enough confidence to celebrate the source. It is in this manner that Professor Flynn has compiled his list of seven men, for he is judging all these men in retrospect; he sees them only from the vantage of living amongst their many lingering effects. Hindsight, however, is a vision easily distorted. Overly impressed by the acclaim that attaches to genius's backwards-looking glance, Professor Flynn adds attributes to his list of seven men that are dubious decorations at best. In addition to suggesting that these are the men of *highest* intelligence, he festoons them also in costumes of wisdom, critical acumen, humane egalitarianism—he turns each into a kind of affable colleague, one that might easily be found just down the university hall. It is in this manner that Professor Flynn demonstrates he does not have an eye for genius as genius truly is, he cannot see genius with a *forwards*-looking glance. Professor Flynn is of the kind—and indeed there are many—who think relativity was first described by a likeable professor of physics, and not by an awkwardly shy patent office clerk.

Pythagoras, Plato, Aristotle, Archimedes, Newton, Gauss, Einstein—

what an unusual collection of men. And unusual not because of their hindsight-regarded achievements, but unusual because in the moment of their catalyzing efforts, each betrayed a set of human characteristics surprisingly troublesome, disruptive and ultimately isolating. From the forwards-looking direction, genius wears a guise exceedingly strange.

In the first place, genius is not in possession of the highest intelligence, genius possesses intelligence only good enough—good enough to be familiar with the environment of the age, for this environment becomes the canvas upon which genius works. But at the margins, genius's intelligence will betray cracks, irritations, dissatisfactions with consensus descriptions; genius's intelligence will score oddly, and not always the best. And in fact, genius remains *closed* to individuals of the highest intelligence: individuals of the highest intelligence are the ones most skilled, most adept at navigating their surroundings as those surroundings *already are*, but those same abilities serve as an impediment to seeing surroundings as they might *possibly be*. For similar reasons, genius remains closed also to groups and teams; the pooling of ideas, even when gathered from the best, reflects the consensus of what is already commonly known, and squelches examination of circumstances yet to be perceived.

To fulfill its revolutionary role, to work its paradigm-shifting magic, to jolt the human species right out of its animal past and into a re-constructed future, genius must remain the province of the individual—the individual acting ruthlessly alone. The introduction of new intelligence into the human environment is not an act of social kindness; the sudden bursting open of new doors to wider and better construction is not a biologically graceful event. This planet passed nearly four billion years without seeing anything remotely similar to the structural re-creation we now can witness all around us—genius has been working in defiance of a well-established norm.

And far from being affable colleagues, individual geniuses are more prone to *turning away* from the common pursuits of their fellow man, are more prone to becoming bitterly and painfully distracted, staring deeply into the patterns and structures of the non-social, non-biological world, teasing from out of those depths the hidden formations that are about to be. Adjectives such as *intelligent, wise, egalitarian, socially graced*—they ring hollow attached to the souls of genius. When we examine more carefully the lives of the seven men on Professor Flynn's list—and indeed when we examine more carefully the characteristics of nearly *all* the geniuses who have graced the human species—we find them much better framed by a more dissonant sounding set of words: brooding, aloof, inscrutable, iconoclastic, temperamental, reticent, compulsive, detached. There is nothing coincidental in these oft-repeated descriptions. Although we have been apt to regard the personality quirks of genius as the result of genius's strain, a deeper understanding of genius's essential task reveals that we have been badly confusing cause and effect. The unusual characteristics of humanity's transformational individuals are not the *result* of genius, they are genius's prerequisite.

And thus we come to autism, that one cognitive paradox Professor Flynn has likely never considered.

Autism is another poorly understood concept in this so-called scientific age. Although autism has been present within humanity for a very long time, its recognition has come only quite recently—a recognition accompanied by grave misunderstandings. In the early twenty-first century, autism is described exclusively as a *medical* condition, observable in children beginning around the age of two or three, characterized by developmental delays, social deficits, language peculiarities, and unusual behaviors and interests. And the assumption of hundreds of research teams, maybe even thousands by now, is that autism's traits are the result of various brain disorders, genetic defects, synaptic abnormalities and environmental toxins—we have become collectively convinced autism is the evidence of something gone terribly wrong. But the blind acceptance of this assumption has resulted in humanity remaining blind to autism's much larger and more positive consequence; for if the day-to-day impact of autism has been to pose unquestionable challenges for the autistic individuals who live within our midst, the era-to-era impact of autism has been to unleash upon the human species the most powerful transformation this planet has ever seen.

Autism's fundamental characteristic is that the individuals possessing this condition do not easily recognize and assimilate to their own species. By contrast, non-autistic individuals—following the well-established biological and evolutionary norm—display from birth a strong, natural affinity for the human features in their surrounding environment; they can easily focus on human faces, quickly respond to human voices, and so on, Non-autistic individuals use this species affinity to gain their sensory grounding—the human environment becomes foreground against a background of sensory noise—and they ride species familiarity into the realms of imitation and assimilation, quickly learning to do what other humans do, swiftly taking their customary place within mankind's domain. Just as bees perceive solely the bee-specific features in their surrounding environment, and thereby learn to behave as bees, just as lions perceive exclusively the lion-specific features in their own surroundings, and thereby assimilate to other lions, so too do humans perceive first and foremost the human-specific features presented all around them, and thereby attach with natural ease to the contours of human existence.

Autistic individuals appear to be the only exception to this species recognition rule. For reasons as yet unknown, autistic individuals fail to gain the same species-specific focus as other humans do, and in consequence chart an entirely different perceptual and developmental course. The challenges are certainly daunting: to varying degree autistic individuals face lifelong struggles to gain sensory, cognitive and biological footing, and for a significant number there will be only limited progress. But counter to prevailing wisdom there are many autistic individuals, most likely a majority, who do make substantial progress by means of an alternative perceptual course, a course that allows them not only to navigate meaningfully their surrounding world, but also to assimilate, if somewhat awkwardly and belatedly, to the human species itself (and thereby explaining how autism, estimated to be present in nearly one percent of the human population, could go entirely unrecognized until as recently as sixty-five years ago).

This alternative perceptual course is the natural response to an autistic individual's initial sensory chaos. Without a human-specific focus to serve for grounding, autistic individuals lack the customary means for determining biological foreground from a background of sensory noise, and thus autistic individuals are threatened right from birth with a massive sensory confusion—and indeed many do experience an assortment of sensory difficulties. Fortunately, not every feature in the surrounding environment presents itself as unbridled noise. In an environment of jumbled auditory impressions, for instance, repeated sounds inherently stand out. In an environment of chaotic visual scenes, symmetry pushes to the front. And in an environment of mostly random events, patterns draw attention. Hungry for signal to relieve the overwhelming rush of sensory noise, autistic individuals focus on environmental features that inherently stand out from the remainder, features rich in those concepts already familiar to this discussion—concepts such as symmetry, pattern, repetition, structure and form. Stymied from the usual course of gaining human-specific perspective, autistic individuals forge their developmental progress by concentrating on non-social, non-biological structure to be found in the world around them. And although some autistic individuals are more successful in this process than others are, although some are quicker, some are slower, although many are drawn to widely varying aspects of a broadly arrayed environment, *all* autistic individuals must crystallize their experience by means of this alternative perceptual course—it becomes, in essence, autism's defining feature.

Strong evidence exists in support of this description of autism, evidence that is abundant, familiar and surprisingly close at hand. The unusual behaviors and interests of autistic children—lining up toys, staring at ceiling fans, twirling, fascination with knobs, buttons, switches, letters, shapes and digits, watching the same video again and again, singing the same song over and over—these activities betray a form of perception noticeably *absent* in social and biological focus, but also noticeably *drawn* to symmetry, repetition and pattern. And these autistic behaviors and interests have not been assimilated from others, they are not the result of human prompting—they have all arisen spontaneously. The unusual routines of autistic children are the natural, indeed the *expected* mode of expression for a form of perception that is engaged primarily by the structural aspects of the non-social, non-biological world.

And of course the irony accompanying these behaviors and interests is that they are so frequently demonized. In our current atmosphere of scientific orthodoxy regarding autism, out of the research community's blind insistence on medicalizing this condition, from humanity's near certitude that autism is the evidence of something gone terribly wrong, autistic behaviors have been decried as symptoms of a mental disease, the destructive by-products of genetic defects and brain dysfunction. Autistic interests have been branded as unworthy, undesirable, unhuman; they are slated again and again for correction, intervention, eradication.

How exceedingly misguided.

In a world in which the human environment has been suddenly and enormously transformed all around us, in a species that has been rapidly progressing from animal to questing knight of a massive universe, in a culture where intelligent men can author books entitled *What is Intelligence?*, and in an era in which the Flynn effect still confounds us as a mystery, how exceedingly misguided to insist on demonizing the behaviors and interests of autistic children—arguably the most natural occurrence of non-biological form and structure being added into the human environment, arguably the most spontaneous occurrence of our expanding human intelligence.

It would be far from unreasonable to conjecture that it must have been around the time of the great leap forward that autistic individuals first gained significant presence within the human population, because it was at that moment evidence begins to appear of their transformational impact. Autistic individuals would have been the first to *notice* the inherent structure contained in the natural world—the geometry of plants, the isomorphisms of natural objects, the logic of the celestial seasons. Only they would have had motivation to embrace such structure, only they would have had need to form their cognitive grounding out of nature's symmetry, repetition and pattern. And from out of those strange new perceptions would have come the many concepts now familiar to the entire species: from symmetry came the concept of space, from repetition came the concept of time, from pattern came the first intimations of logic and mathematics. And alongside the introduction of such new concepts would have arisen also the need for language; for with the human world now bursting its biologically immediate bonds and reaching across realms of time and space in which to explore, there was now the need for a representational intermediary to help bridge that expanding conceptual gap.

This process of human transformation would have been slow and uncertain over the course of many millennia—by current standards of human environmental change, fifty thousand years is an immensely long period of time—but increasingly able to perceive non-biological structure and form within their surroundings, more and more capable of re-creating similar structural effects, humans began adding a plethora of formative artifacts into their expanding world and grew ever more intelligent with each new addition. By the era of ancient Greece we can perceive the outline of a now increasingly familiar story: the unusual members of that society, the near outcasts such as Pythagoras, the ones barely attached such as Socrates and Archimedes, positing strange new descriptions of their surrounding universe, offering up strange new methods of calculation and logical discourse, envisioning strange new contraptions with which to re-create again and again and again. We know only bits and pieces about the four Greeks on Professor Flynn's list, but filling in with traits from the list's more modern members, we can reasonably surmise all the unifying characteristics: late- or strange-talking, socially awkward, irascible, obsessed with structure, compelled by form, unusually—not greatly—intelligent. As has been always the case, in famous ways we now celebrate in retrospect and by more subtle means now long forgotten, genius has arisen out of a mode of perception quite unlike the human biological norm.

And even today, even in the modern world, even with so much intelligence now embodied into our human environment, even with the templates of scientific method and artistic technique made available to nearly all—even today, genius remains the more natural domain of the autistic individual. Tomorrow's transformational vision will be derived by the one least attached to the common perceptions of today. Our continuing medicalization of autism, our insistent demonization of autism's spontaneous effect—this form of blindness carries the danger of an unforeseen consequence. Because the cure of autism will not be the end of a tragic brain disorder; the eradication of autism will not mean the passing of a troubling mental disease. The removal of autism from the entire human species will produce only a bitterly ironic solution to the mystery of our expanding human intelligence—it will produce the ignoble end to the Flynn effect.

I continue to maintain a large degree of respect and gratitude for Professor Flynn and his work. His tireless promulgation of what has come to be known as the Flynn effect has been a research achievement of no small significance, a rare jewel of discovery that has jolted us right out of our accustomed way of seeing things, thereby leading to broadly expanded horizons. The only accomplishment I can think of to liken it to would be the Michelson-Morley experiment with its steadfast denial of the luminiferous ether, eventually paving the way to relativity.

But as grateful as I am to Professor Flynn for his namesake discovery, I am as equally dismayed by his book *What is Intelligence?* I am especially disappointed in its clumsy, unconvincing attempts to explain the Flynn effect away. The book seems uninspired, shoddily organized, poorly reasoned, badly edited, and is transparent in only one respect—it makes it all too abundantly clear that Professor Flynn does not realize the significance of what he has himself discovered, he does not have a keen enough eye for the Flynn effect's broadly expanded horizons. Michelson and Morley too, I would note, puzzled by their own unexpected results, made several attempts in later life to rationalize their findings away, none of these efforts ever redounding to either one's credit. Data is data. When confronted by data that runs counter to our accustomed way of seeing things, we as humans have but two choices: we can try to explain the results away, or we can change our perceptions of the experienced world. The former choice paves the all-too-common road of modern academic science; the latter, as described above, walks the more promising path of genius.

Intelligence, genius, and autism—the common understandings of each of these constructs must fall. Intelligence is not the by-product of our biochemical brain, it is instead the harvest of the structured world we have been building around us. Genius is not the title to be conferred upon higher intelligence, it is instead the catalyst prompting human intelligence to grow. Autism is not a mental illness, not a brain disorder, it is instead the source of humanity's changing perception of its experienced world—it is, with care and understanding, genius's formative soil.

Echolalia

Echolalia, an early warning sign of ...

I can almost hear a savannah-bound animal through the not-so-distant murmur of time, but the static has grown unusually thick today and has taken on strange and hypnotic form: chants of war, rosary prayers begging for peace; tragedy and comedy built around chorus and refrain; the watchmen crying the cycling hours, tribal histories passed down as sung recipe; the recitation of poetry and its beguiling trick of rhyme; and finally those incessant, relentless demands for justice—the repeated rhetorical rapture of "I have a dream."

Echolalia, an early warning sign of ... a language *dis*ability?

Spinning and Twirling

Spinning and twirling, an early warning sign of ...

I can almost reach a savannah-bound animal through the not-so-long funnel of time, but vertigo has overwhelmed my senses today, I am taken by such strange and dizzying form: the potter's wheel turned by skillful hands, the joiner's swiftly circular blade; cathedral domes, intricate clocks, mills forever grinding (all those cogs and pulleys and gears); one bouncing ball past the merry-go-round, satellites in orbit; Euclid's compass, Euler's pi, and a Copernican revolution so perfect it might leave you longing for an ideal, heavenly sphere.

Spinning and twirling, an early warning sign of ... a *defect*?

Lining Up Toys

Lining up toys, an early warning sign of …

I can almost see a savannah-bound animal through the not-so-distant mist of time, but the fog has dawned unusually dense today and has taken on strange and net-like form: endless beads tied upon endless strings, countless wheat planted row after row after row; road and track and wire gridded for mile upon mile upon mile; city block connected to city block, house abutting house; millions of books upon thousands of shelves (letter attached to letter, line after line after line); assembly plants running straight as an arrow from entry door to exit, and people queued up everywhere to acquire item after item after item.

Lining up toys, an early warning sign of … a *disorder?*

Early Warning Signs

The following two assumptions enjoy widespread acceptance within the academic and research communities:

- Human intelligence is centered within the structures and dynamics of the human brain.
- The unusual early behaviors of autistic children (for example, lining up toys, echolalia, spinning and twirling) are the indicators of a neurological disorder.

But I would have us consider an alternative view of both human intelligence and these so-called early warning signs of autism; because not only are the above two assumptions false, their negations directly support each other.

It has become tantamount to dogma within the scientific community that human intelligence is centered within the human brain, and I am certain I will not make the slightest dent in that conviction anytime soon. Armed with ever more sophisticated brain imaging technology and fortressed by countless experiments attempting to match neuronal activation to a plethora of human tasks, the world of cognitive research expects soon to discover the exact neuronal location of logic, language and the arts, and hopes not long after to describe all the intellectual mechanisms pulling together this tangle of synapses, cortices, and brain matter plasticity. The neuroimaging pictures are indeed vibrant, and the metrics are certainly bountiful; but conceptually, I am convinced all is not well.

Consider the hallmark features of human intelligence—pattern recognition, sophisticated visual-spatial capacity, conceptual logic, mathematical and musical skill, the pragmatic use of abstract language. Does it strike no scientist as even the slightest bit unnerving that these features first made their appearance only quite recently in human history? Almost nothing of what we take and measure for human intelligence today can be found in the behaviors of *Homo sapiens* from just thirty to fifty thousand years ago, and it was only the slightest hint of such ability that began to emerge near the dawn of recorded time.

We gaze with anticipation into our fMRIs and we calculate hopefully all our degrees of significance, but we forget that we peer not just into the brains of our contemporaries, but also into the brains of our more distant ancestors. Thus we must ask—why the sudden and late emergence of all this cranial intelligence for which we so fervently delve? Why could we not have built our modern civilizations way back then, when these same brain structures and capacities already existed? Why did this species tarry until just so recently?

And of course there is that little detail known as the Flynn effect, the observation that intelligence scores have been increasing at roughly three IQ points per decade. What a puzzler that discovery must be for any neuronal-based model of human intelligence, and no wonder those who have staked considerable reputations on such models—including Professor Flynn himself—seem so willing to explain this phenomenon away as mostly a twentieth-century anomaly, one soon to dissipate (demonstrating again that today's scientist stands far more ready to embrace an unlikely coincidence than question the foundations of an established career).

Me, I would much rather be bold. I would rather negate that first assumption, and place the locus of human intelligence firmly *outside* the human skull.

If instead of sourcing human intelligence within the human brain, we distribute it throughout the environmental structures we humans have been building all around us, then we arrive at a tangible locale for intelligence that more directly fits what we already know. Tens of thousands of years ago, the human environment was almost entirely biological, and so were the forms of our human intellect: food acquisition, shelter, warmth, sex, avoidance of deadly enemies—these were the sum cognitive focus of a species whose universe extended no farther than the boundaries of the tribe. No clocks, no yardsticks, no musical notes, no truth functions deciding yea and nay; not on the hunter-gatherer's grassy plain. Today, and quite suddenly, we no longer live on that plain—our locale has been dramatically shifted, growing both larger and more detailed in ways we have scarcely begun to conceive. And it is no mere coincidence that as our settings have been so dramatically transformed, so have the forms and degrees of our intelligence. With our surroundings now overflowing with structure, pattern, complexity, repetition, embodied conceptualization—much of it decidedly non-biological—our abilities to navigate and master this strange new world are exactly the same skill sets we measure when we place a human being in front of that little booklet called an IQ exam.

It is not our brain that has been changing—there has not passed nearly enough evolutionary time for that. The human brain, plasticity and all, has grown not one iota smarter; for the human brain is not the seat of human intelligence. It is our physical environment—*that* is the tangible object that has turned so remarkably more brilliant. The *form* of our physical human surroundings—there can be found the long sought-after location of our increasing cognitive skills.

And the Flynn effect? The Flynn effect resolves into little more than a tautology under this new paradigm of intelligence, for it becomes simply another measure of the increasing amount of pattern and complexity we humans have been embodying into our environment year after year, along with the confirmation that each generation absorbs this strange new information and its mostly non-biological form. Each succeeding generation finds itself born into a set of surroundings more complex, more detailed, more rapid than those perceived by the previous generations, and by necessity learns to navigate and to master, and lo and behold finds itself scoring better than all its progenitors on any test designed to capture intelligence. The Flynn effect is not a twentieth-century coincidence; it is not produced by better nutrition, selective breeding or a socially-driven multiplier effect (and Professor Flynn, it is most certainly *not* produced by proximity to the local college). The Flynn effect has been with us from the time of the great leap forward, and assuming we can learn to embrace this phenomenon, instead of so glibly dismiss it, the Flynn effect can remain with us, and sustain us, for a considerable time to come.

But I can hear your objections in my ear already: have I not placed the cart well before the horse? The essential question, you say, is not that we humans have been constructing a structurally more complex environment, and have been learning to live more skillfully within it—anyone can agree to that—the essential question, you say, is what *produced* this remarkable transformation? Are not the splendors of modern civilization the unquestionable *result* of human intelligence, are they not the obvious evidence of its cranial existence?

Well, having absorbed enough logic from the current environment to know that I would not want to be accused of placing a cart well before a horse, let me state unequivocally that it was *not* preexisting neuronal intelligence that prompted the massive environmental transformation. If it is a *cause* of human intelligence that we are seeking, then we must direct our attention *outside* intelligence and search for that catalyst someplace else. So let me turn this discussion to what must seem to be a completely different topic—let us consider the early warning signs of autism.

Within the autism research community, the early behaviors of autistic children have been branded with the most dreadful of reputations, and I am certain I will not prompt the slightest pause in that practice anytime soon. Tarnished with such adjectives as *obsessive, worthless, aberrant,* autistic behaviors have been cast into one of the psychiatric community's most profitable and prolific targets, an abundantly fertile field for the development of eradicating therapies, minimalizing drugs, and the not-so-occasional slur. The funding grants are indeed impressive, and the size of the research teams has certainly grown massive; but conceptually, I am convinced all is not well.

Consider the *form* of those early autistic behaviors—lining up objects, repeating verbal or sung passages, fascination with circles, letters and numbers, turning on and off light switches, rocking, spinning, all the rest. Does it strike no researcher as even the slightest bit unnerving that these behaviors are in no way random or chaotic, that these behaviors cluster yet again and again around the concepts of pattern, logic, repetition and symmetry? Tens of thousands of years ago such concepts had barely scratched the human surface; it was only quite recently such features were embraced by this species as the ones making us distinctly noble. And yet we confidently pronounce autistic behaviors as aberrant, we calculate with smug certainty their substantial difference from the norm, all the while conveniently forgetting that we as *Homo sapiens* have been jolted quite suddenly into being nothing like our normal animal selves. So I must ask, why the contemptuous dismissal of these distinctive behaviors we have not yet begun to fathom? Why, given our lingering uncertainty about the exact location and genesis of human intelligence—why are we so intent on demonizing what is arguably the most spontaneous occurrence of intellect's most fundamental form?

And of course there is that little detail known as the brilliant autistic outcome, the growing evidence that many autistic individuals can achieve remarkable potential, display unique and surprising ability, mature to lives of stunning productivity—all without the benefit of psychotropic drugs, biomedical treatments or behavior-altering therapies (and some, dare I even suggest this, achieving such outcomes *despite* such interventions). What a puzzler those outcomes must be for any disorder-based model of autism, and little wonder those who have staked considerable livelihoods on such models, almost the entire research community it would appear, are hurrying to explain such individuals away—as trivial by-products, as insignificant anomalies, as outliers to be ignored (demonstrating again that today's scientist stands far more ready to slander an experimental subject than jeopardize the source of any funding).

Me, I would much rather be bold. I would rather negate that second assumption, and place the early behaviors of autistic children firmly *outside* the category of neurological disorder.

If instead of classifying autism as cognitive damage, we consider it to be an alternative and valid form of cognitive perception, then we arrive at a catalyst for human intelligence that does not require the explanatory magic of a nearly instantaneous neurological or genetic transformation. What better, and more natural, means to jolt a species from its strictly biological gaze than to have appear among it members with a decidedly different point of view—now in addition to concerns of food, sex and enemies, there can appear those creeping influences of symmetry, pattern, repetition and form. Through a lack of species recognition, the early perceptions of autistic children become the counterpart to species learning; they arise from a spontaneous need to make sense of experience not well grounded in biological imitation. And thus autistic perception, and the behavior resulting from it, opens windows onto concepts mankind has never considered before, opens windows onto the myriad instances of non-biological form. This collision of autistic and non-autistic perspectives has been many times awkward, no one would argue that; and the difficulties of autistic individuals have been many times onerous, that is not something to be denied. But apologies are not required, and neither are the slanders, for the blended results have been astonishingly prodigious, or had you failed to notice? Are we not all of us, autistic and non-autistic alike, are we not suddenly departed from the hunter-gatherer's grassy plain?

Autistic perception is not an affliction, that dogma has badly missed the mark. The study of autism as mental illness has produced not one iota of understanding for this species-changing condition. Autism itself is the key, the key to mankind's physically constructed intelligence. Autistic perspectives, *they* are what has prompted our environment's massive structural change. There can be found the long sought-for genesis of our increasing cognitive skills.

And the brilliant autistic outcome? It resolves into little more than expectation under this new paradigm of autism, for it becomes the confirmation that autistic influences have been working transformationally among us for a very long time. Before this species "discovered" mental illness, before it began suffocating unique perspectives under medications and behavior-altering sessions, the vast majority of autistic individuals matured quietly and productively among us, they etched their strangely patterned perceptions into mankind's fast-transfiguring path. And as each human generation found itself born into surroundings embodying more and more of these strangely patterned perceptions—and by necessity learned to navigate and master—lo and behold humanity found itself fast abandoning the strictures of its evolutionary past and fast constructing the intelligence of its future. Autism is not a twentieth-century emergence; it is not the by-product of industrial toxins, genetic defects or brain dysfunctions (and it is most certainly *not* a condition to be drugged and therapied away). Autism has been among us from the time of the great leap forward, and assuming we can learn to embrace this phenomenon, instead of so harshly dismiss it, the benefits of autism can remain with us, and sustain us, for a considerable time to come.

But I know all this must sound so absurdly impossible, and really, I know no one is currently listening.

So for now I will leave all the researchers to their neuroimaging equipment—I understand how giddy they must be with excitement and what a pretty penny they have paid for the privilege, so I would not dream of distracting them from these momentary pursuits. But after all their picture taking is over, after all their statistical packages have been run, after they have written all the same tired conclusions to all the same tired assumptions, if perhaps a scientist or two should find themselves suddenly grown weary, perhaps a little discouraged, should they think maybe a brief respite or a change of scenery might do them a little good, I would be happy to guide them to the room one over, the one where their experimental subjects bide their time by playing on the floor—lining up toys, echoing passages, spinning and twirling. And I promise I will be gentle with my suggestion, in fact I will just barely whisper it into their ear, that perhaps this is what they have been looking for all along, right here before their eyes—these early warning signs of a dawning human intelligence.

Intelligent Design

William Dembski, he of intelligent design fame, has written a poignant account (Dembski 2008) of taking his autistic son to a gathering run by a popular faith healer in the hopes of obtaining some miraculous autism healing—a healing which, as events turned out, would not even be offered, let alone consummated. The faith healer of course revealed himself as little more than a conjurer of theater and coinage; and after having endured the multi-hour ordeal of a long drive, a needless wait, blaringly loud music and the insipid amusements of a traveling medicine show, Mr. Dembski's wife and autistic son, summoned at long last to approach the stage for some personal healing and prayer, found themselves more than an hour later effectively shunned and turned away. The entire family drove home bitterly disappointed, if somewhat wiser about the nature of popular revivalist gatherings.

In many ways, Mr. Dembski's account is one of the more moving articles I have read in recent years, and this coming from a man for whom I share hardly a thread of common understanding. But if Mr. Dembski and I share little in the way of a common philosophical background, we do share a commonality of experience, for I too have an autistic son, one of nearly the same age as Mr. Dembski's. Thus I can commiserate completely. In fact, I cannot help but be touched greatly by Mr. Dembski's story and cannot help but feel within the very depths of my soul the bitter anguish and confusion that must have been experienced during that distressing ordeal. But of course it is not *Mr. Dembski's* anguish and confusion I am feeling—I am feeling the anguish and confusion that must have been experienced by his autistic son.

It is an oft-told story: salvation was at hand—so remarkably close at hand—if only it had been recognized and accepted.

There was indeed a miracle being offered to Mr. Dembski at that revivalist gathering, a miracle offered so quietly, so humbly, so simply, that amidst all the dancing, all the singing, all the hearty exhortations— and amidst all the tinkling of collection plates—it must have gone so easily overlooked. The miracle being offered to Mr. Dembski on that bitterly ironic night occurred at the very moment of his autistic son's rejection (and how Christianly ironic is that?), just one more rejection in a long line of rejections—from doctors, from school administrators, from nearly the entire human community, and (dare he confess it) from Mr. Dembski himself. But at the very moment of that one further rejection, the forced turning away from that popular minister of god and the turning back towards a reassessing father—now *there* was a moment worthy of a hallelujah chorus.

And to Mr. Dembski's credit, at least on this particular occasion, he was not entirely immune to the poignancy and gift of that telling moment. Quietly accepting his autistic son back into the family fold, driving his children home at that ungodly hour, waiting until each had fallen asleep to share with his wife the doubts now arising within his troubled soul, Mr. Dembski had taken those first, faltering steps towards the altar of his *own* salvation—hallelujah, indeed.

But how to encourage him to take all the remaining steps? How to inspire him to face all the challenges yet to come? Do we dare to remind Mr. Dembski that in the story he cares about most, the father does not reject the unwanted son.

If there is an entity deserving of the name *God*, then that entity must exist in the here and now, and I do not mean in the here and now of any particular church, I mean in the here and now of each and every moment. The discovery and acceptance of this world as this world truly is—not as we humans desire or demand it to be—there can be found the glory behind both science and religion. And accepting autism for what it is, welcoming both its offbeat demands as well as its profoundly transformational impact upon the entire human species—there might be found the admittedly narrow path that one day uplifts all mankind.

Let Mr. Dembski begin his reconstructed catechism with that lesson and that lesson alone. And after he has begun to master it, after he has incorporated it deeply within his being, only then might I be willing to sit and talk with him about something worthy of being called *intelligent design*.

Mathematical Weaknesses

Here is a telling statement by Professor Carl B. Boyer straight from—of all places—*A History of Mathematics* (Boyer 1968):

> "A number of deficiencies in pre-Hellenic mathematics are quite obvious. Extant papyri and tablets contain specific cases and problems only, with no general formulations, and one may question whether these early civilizations really appreciated the unifying principles that are at the core of mathematics."

Well, of course. But then again: *one may question* whether academicians can see beyond the end of their own nose.

The Context of Neuroimaging

One does not understand an accounting program by taking electronic measurement of all the chips, wires and disks. Strangely enough, one needs to know something about accounting before any of those readings make sense.

Searle

Another of Derrida's non-identical twins.
So many approachable works—
Like a stash of Chrysler building replicas
Fashioned from styrofoam blocks.
(And it must be admitted,
There is a certain amount of talent
Required for a portfolio like that.
And it must be admitted,
The graduate school audiences
Prefer their buildings that way.)

Of course the trouble with approachable works
Is they dare an approach,
And up close,
We see no business is ever conducted in a building like that—
No elevators rising and falling,
No boardroom dramas between dusk and dawn,
No graphite pencils ground to their messy point.
Up close,
It resembles not a building at all—
For that, one keeps a safer distance.

Far removed from campus,
The child without siblings,
The child without peers,
Dares to slice the styrofoam to ribbons,
Crushes the blocks for pellets,
Burns the plastic down to goo,
And beyond that flotsam books uncertain passage
Over fathom-rich seas.
Searle (your brethren too)—
It is of no use to craft life preservers
From the material of a philosophy professor's chair.

The Philosophy of Academic Philosophy

Do academic philosophers write about anything besides other philosophers? Kripke, Dummett, Foucault, Wright, Rawls, the list goes on and on. Like denizens of a closed-off room, these dilettantes can breathe only their self-made stench.

Open a window, for God's sake! Out in the sunshine you might find Thoreau, Kierkegaard, Nietzsche, Wittgenstein—all romping about, and giving a rat's ass for their fellow philosophers. But no, behind these heavy curtains we find Dennett, Searle, Rorty—each waxing ad nauseam on … Dennett, Searle, Rorty (not to mention, waxing ad nauseam on Thoreau, Kierkegaard, Nietzsche, Wittgenstein).

Why would anyone strive to become a philosopher for the purpose of regurgitating other philosophers? Can these professors not think for themselves?

Maybe Derrida, you say—maybe he is the exception. Well, here too we are stuck in the morass of other philosophers, although I admit the *approach* is unique. But what can it say about modern philosophy to know that its con artists are the most creative?

What If the Flynn Effect Has Ended?

Some recent studies have suggested that the Flynn effect might soon be ending, at least in the Scandinavian countries, and several authors, including Professor Flynn himself, seem to have latched onto this possibility like it were a lifeline being tossed to a drowning man. Those who have been regarding the Flynn effect as mostly a twentieth-century phenomenon, an historical anomaly as it were, must be experiencing near palpable relief at this hint the anomaly might soon be fading away. Such a disappearance would end their fright, would end their gnawing fear that mankind is indeed growing ruthlessly more intelligent in a damn near inexplicable way.

But some of us are not so easily frightened.

Those of us who have contemplated the entire history of mankind, from its animal-like existence of not that long ago, through the sudden sprouting of complex civilizations beginning around six thousand years ago, to the franticly paced modern efforts to transform nearly every square inch of this entire planet (and to those of us who have seen the imprint of the Flynn effect *throughout* that blazing history), any suggestion that the Flynn effect might soon be ending—and coincidentally just now, right at the very moment of its discovery—well, how are we to choke back our reaction without offending those who have become so terribly frightened? For really, such a suggestion is little more than laughable.

To be sure, over the past fifty thousand years the Flynn effect has passed through many surges and ebbs. To focus on Western civilization alone, the era of Ancient Greece, along with its enduring aftermath, was undoubtedly one of those periods during which the Flynn effect ran at peak. One glance at the physical constructions of that age—the buildings, the written mathematics, the crafted and portrayed arts— one sees embodiment of pattern and form going far beyond anything mankind had ever experienced before. That embodiment, suffused throughout the populace and handed down through the generations, showered its re-creating and foundational intelligence across the Roman empire and well into the first millennium A.D., and it was not until the stretch of Dark and Middle Ages that we can discern a slowing down of this orderly construction—and even then only a slowing down, not a complete halting. Western civilization at 1500 A.D. was still more rapid and complex than Western civilization at 500 A.D., and elsewhere of course—in Byzantium, India, China—we find yet more examples of the Flynn effect crescendoing into various bursts of sudden and local bloom.

Beginning with the Renaissance, the pace of structural change embodied into the human environment resumed once more a rapid acceleration, and over the last five hundred years and across all manner of civilization, man's temporal, spatial, and non-biological capacities have increased at a nearly breakneck speed. The intelligence tests of the twentieth century have captured only the most recent period of this long-running phenomenon; if there had been intelligence tests available during all the previous centuries, the Flynn effect would have been discovered well before now. Professor Flynn has not stumbled onto anything new, he has stumbled only onto the most recent evidence of a process that has been profoundly reshaping the human landscape from the time of the great leap forward. And if the impressive Flynn effect statistics from the twentieth century are to be telling us anything at all, it is that from sheer momentum alone, the Flynn effect can be expected to remain with us, and sustain us, for a considerable time to come.

But allow me to offer a moment's respite for those who are so terribly frightened. Let us consider, for speculation's sake, what would happen if indeed the Flynn effect has ended. What this implies of course is that in theory any one of us should be able to score as well on a future-offered intelligence test (say those being sat for two hundred years hence) as we might tally on the currently offered standardized forms. This feat, we realize in retrospect, would have been far beyond the capacity of those poor souls who lived in the early nineteenth century; for try imagining a man from the early 1800s suddenly nabbed by the scruff of his neck, hustled forward a couple hundred years or so, whisked by airplane, taxi and elevator to the brightly lit, sharply cornered examination room, placed before that typed-out pamphlet of the strangest looking shapes, the most oddly worded phrases, pen and stopwatch waiting impatiently on the table beside him. What answers are we to anticipate from this nineteenth-century man, what brilliance might we soon expect to hear, beyond, that is, his repeated stammering, "But dear sir, what exactly are you proposing I do?"

Respite over. For honestly how are we to believe—frightened or not—that we ourselves can escape a similar fate? Try imagining yourself suddenly bolted forward to the twenty-third century, hastened to an examination hall by powered means you cannot even begin to fathom, suddenly strapped to a contraption of all manner of knobs and wires and switches (or at least, those are the only words you can think of to describe them), and now with flashes of multi-dimensional light dancing all around you, with rapid questions being poured upon you in grammars you have never considered before, all the while accompanied by frantic demands to respond with a quick jab of finger, a flicker of eyelid once or twice, or at least a simple grunt or two. And just about the time you have managed to catch your breath, just about the time you have gathered enough wits about you to offer at least one feeble attempt at a reasonable answer, the lights of the examination hall suddenly darken, the rapid stream of questions comes to a jarring halt, and from out of the walls the stentorian, twenty-third century form of a tut-tut voice announces that your time has ended and that your score has failed to register, at least on any significant range. Some intellect you turned out to be.

If the Flynn effect has ended, then so has the course of human progress. To embrace such an absurdity would be to misperceive what the Flynn effect has been trying to tell us, it would be to misconceive Professor Flynn's question, *What is intelligence?* There are no paradoxes to be explained away from increasing intelligence scores, there are only the befuddlements of brain science dogmas—the ones that have been turning our inquiries outside in. The Flynn effect compels us to remove intelligence from out of our brain and place it in surroundings where it more rightly belongs, place it in the structured landscapes we humans have been building all around us and will continue to build for a considerable time to come. A world increasingly more spatial, more temporal. An environment always more patterned, more frenzied. And what wonder can it be that we require newer generations to absorb each change afresh, and leave all the ancestors behind?

It is not the Flynn effect that should be frightening us, but rather its end.

The Flynn effect has been shadowing the path of the human journey, it has measured the pace of our considerable progress, it has taken us all the way from savannah-bound primate to questing knight of a massive universe. Do not seek intelligence in packets of scores alone; do not confine intelligence to the prison of the human brain. Cast your eye wider, cast your eye across history's entire vista—from horse-drawn buggies to rockets in flight, from ground-hugging hovels to skyscrapers knifing air, from flints and shovels and axes to computers and networks and drones. Cast your eye across that entire scene, then say with conviction that the show is about to end. No, the sudden halt would jolt us right out of our skin; the end of the Flynn effect can only mean the death knell of all mankind. Allow me to save my fright for that possibility alone, for humanity's darkest age indeed.

Language

How Traditional Speech Therapy Can Help the Autistic Child

When my autistic son was not quite four years old he began weekly speech therapy, an hour each Wednesday afternoon. Often I would pick him up from these appointments, and thus I would get to hear the report of how well—or how poorly—the session had gone. Maybe it was my imagination, but I swear those reports sounded exactly the same from week to week. The therapist would always begin her summary by opening the same three-ring binder, the stock tool of her trade, the one stuffed with page after faded page of cartoon-rendered social scenes. And from what I could gather, Brian was being made to sit at a table the entire time and was being made to listen as the therapist would narrate each illustration in increasing detail and then was being scored on how well he would answer questions about what he had seen and heard—multiple points for answers with words, fewer points for answers by gesture, and of course zero points for silence or an inappropriate response. "I couldn't seem to get his attention today," the therapist would finally say. "He kept getting distracted by the fan."

It was summertime when Brian took those sessions, and the therapist's office was part of a sprawling complex that like everything else needed to be cooled. So upon walking out the door an inevitable question would always arise at my side: "Go see air conditioners?"

"Sure, Brian, we can go see air conditioners."

And off he would careen, steering an uneasy path to that first buzzing box, and he would approach all these metallic idols with the same intense, corner-of-the-eye stare, hands clasped tightly, shoulders scrunching back and forth. "Lift you up?" he would ask pronoun-reversally in front of each one, and I would lift him up to verify the status of the spinning or not-yet-spinning blades. "It is on, it is off," he would pronounce with such simple solemnity. And this he would follow with a ritual counting of all the air conditioners in each row, and next a litany of all their colors, and finally a desperate, yet eloquent pleading to let him go see at least one more—in all, a full half-hour deluge from a chattering autistic storm.

That is how traditional speech therapy can help the autistic child.

Language Acquisition

Noam Chomsky argued that the speed at which young children acquire language—which is indeed impressive—supports the idea that language must be an instinct in humans. But Chomsky failed to appreciate the speed at which the *species itself* acquired language—even more impressive, and a fatal blow to any talk about language instincts.

What most children have an instinct for is to do what other humans do.

The Prerequisites of Language

Nearly all animal species have sufficient biological equipment for the production of abstract language—they can make sounds, they can gesture, they can rub against one another. Heck, with access to something as simple as mud, most organisms could write things down.

As we humans have by now so ably demonstrated, nearly any physical artifact can serve the purpose of conveying language. What other animals *lack* is not the biological or physical means for language, but instead what language *represents*. For what good is an abstract language when one's entire world is already present? What good is an abstract language when one's entire existence is always in the here and now?

And we humans too—we had nothing to talk about until just so recently.

Language and Biological Immediacy

Language is the use of a biologically immediate artifact to represent something not biologically immediate.

All biological organisms, including humans, experience their existence *only* within biological immediacy. That which is removed in space, that which is remote in time, that which is not directly accessible through immediate biological capacity—such events cannot be directly engaged or experienced by any biological organism. Each sensation, each urge, each reaction transpires in the here and now—there is no alternative available, that is the fundamental nature of biological experience.

And indeed, until just recently on this planet, that has been the fundamental *limit* of biological experience.

Although a biological organism has no means to remove itself from its biological immediacy, humans have demonstrated that organisms can use the *material* of biological immediacy to represent something which *is* removed, to represent something not biologically immediate. In this manner, language serves as a bridge to conceptual realms that would be otherwise unreachable. Using language, a biological organism can remain within the compulsory confines of its biological immediacy while using the artifacts *inside* that biological immediacy—the material of language—to represent that which is *beyond* biological immediacy.

The material of language can be almost anything, the choice is entirely arbitrary. Humans began naturally enough with gestures and vocalizations but have recently adopted a wide assortment of materials that can be touched, seen, heard and transported across distance and interval. What remains transformational and crucial about language is not the material being used but instead the elements and structure being represented—events of space, time and other non-biological, patterned conceptualizations. Although a biological organism can never directly engage such elements (because they are biologically removed), it can use the representational accuracy of language to help navigate these elements nonetheless, and thereby change the course and circumstances of its own biological experience. Humans have been engaging in such activities with an ever increasing fervor over the past several thousand years, and with the aid of language, while still confined within the limits of their biological immediacy, humans have been rapidly freeing themselves from the restrictions of their evolutionary, animal past.

If one wants to understand the origins and structure of language, one must focus not exclusively on the material of language, since that material is completely arbitrary; and one goes even further afield to focus on mentalizations and brain processes, since these mentalizations are little more than the re-creation of the material of language itself. If one wants to understand the origins and structure of language, one focuses instead on the non-biological elements being represented, and wonders about their sudden appearance on this planet and about their peculiar form. After all, this planet passed more than four billion years without any species ever considering time, space or any other non-immediate concept; and humans too, they passed tens of thousands of years completely oblivious to anything outside their immediate biological experience.

Keep this in mind: that which is far removed from biological immediacy is also far removed from normal biological perception.

Phantom of the Pinker

Is our tool use mental? Do we humans toil with hammers, saws and wrenches because we *thought them up* at some point? Is there a specific brain module for each tool—a screwdriver module, a lathe module—or is there just one all-purpose brain module covering tool use in general?

Or does all this talk of tool-specific brain modules sound rather silly? And if so, ask yourself why we take this approach seriously for language.

Humans now have many distinct forms of language, but each form manifests itself as a physical and immediate artifact—sound vibrations, movements of fingers, marks on a page, switches in computer memory. Although I can *imagine* a spoken conversation, I can do so only because I have already *experienced* such conversations, they have actually existed in my physical and immediate reality—just like hammers, saws and wrenches.

When we describe language as mental we get distracted from what language actually is, and dreaming up language modules for the human brain sounds like the work of someone confused by what exists right before his very eyes.

Anti-Evolution

At the time of the great leap forward, Steven A. Pinker, with nothing amiss in genes, neurons, brain or ego, fails to graduate high school, fails to earn an advanced degree, fails to publish a single word, fails to gain appointment to any prestigious institutions, and fails to comprehend the first clue as to why.

Fifty thousand years later, all is rectified—except of course the latter.

Linguistics for Autistics

Language is the use of a biologically immediate artifact to represent something not biologically immediate.

Almost any material artifact can serve the purpose of conveying language—gestures, sound, nudges, smears in the mud. The larynx was convenient, but not essential.

Since the locus of language is the external, material world (not the inside of our human skull) language remains open to any life-form. If a species does not use language, it is because that species has nothing to say.

Humans had nothing to say for an incredibly long period of time—this species passed the better part of its existence locked inside its biological immediacy.

What is crucial about language is not its *material* form, but rather its *representational* form. That is what connects biological immediacy to conceptual distance.

If you are aware of a pattern, then you are aware of time. If you are aware of symmetry, then you are aware of space. But how do you inform your neighbor?

Among other things, language was a solution to autistic loneliness.

One cannot deceive within one's own biological immediacy. Deception is a consequence of language.

Not only is deception a consequence of language, it is an essential *feature* of language. The means by which one conveys biologically removed events are also the means by which one conveys biologically removed *non*-events.

As with nearly every other autism-inspired invention, non-autistics quickly co-opted language for their own use and bent it to their own purpose. And as with nearly every other instance of non-autistic pilferage, the results have been stunningly prodigious.

Chomsky was doing just fine when he approached linguistics as a branch of logic. He went awry when he began approaching linguistics as a branch of science.

The underlying structure of language (Chomsky's universal grammar) reflects the structure of the non-biological world: space and time, stasis and change, mass and energy. The underlying structure of language arises from autistic perception.

Language always acts (represents) in the here and now. Persistent forms of language—such as writing—convey the material of language across space and time, but the sending and receiving still occur within someone's biological immediacy.

Although autistic perception launched human language and gave it its underlying structure, non-autistic perception soon provided a hefty adornment—language gained its biological and social girth practically overnight.

Pronouns are superfluous to language, as is gender—but try convincing the ninety-nine percent who would feel empty without them.

What value is *you* and *I*, *we* and *they*, *he*, *she* and *it*, when a proper noun would serve just as well? (That is a question asked by someone not strongly attached to the species.)

Small talk is a reminder of this species' former days, when language itself would have been superfluous. Subtext was once all we had, and all we needed.

Autistic children grow up to a language that has been corrupted—the biological and social adornments constantly throw them off.

Autistic and non-autistic individuals are both exceedingly logical—just not in the same way.

Mathematics, logic, science—these are all salves against deception, and as such belong under the umbrella of language, not the umbrella of the objective world.

An artifact of language can be used to represent language itself, but it is almost never wise to do so. Meta-language is a misuse of the tool.

Language is not an instinct. Even less so is it a *human* instinct. What most children have an instinct for is to do what other humans do.

There are no language modules inside the human brain—just the magical thinking modules of linguistics professors and cognitive scientists.

Together with self-reflecting mirrors and obsessive masturbators, Steven Pinker reminds us that expansive vision is possible only because cognitively diverse people have the wherewithal to get beyond themselves.

The Dual Root of Human Language

Human language has shot forth from two distinct roots, from two very different sources of fundamental influence.

The first source has been the temporal, spatial and logistical pattern that constitutes the order of the surrounding, non-biological world. This influence is seen most clearly in language's underlying structure: object and concept, noun and verb, temporal tenses, spatial adjectives, all manner of nuanced prepositional form. This aspect of language did not arise from humanity's biological and evolutionary past, but instead originated from the struggles of this species' unusual interloper—it came from the autistic perceptions and cognitions that gained significant foothold within the human population. Autistic individuals, not cognitively grounded by the usual species-centered perceptions, create cognitive grounding instead out of the patterns and symmetries to be found within the surrounding environment. But since autistic individuals are biological creatures themselves, and since they have need to convey their unique form of perception both to themselves and to others, they have uncovered also the means by which biologically remote perception can be represented *within* one's own biological immediacy—they have uncovered that essential accompaniment called language.

And yet, as has happened on so many other occasions of autistic discovery and invention, language was quickly adopted, transformed and widely spread by the more numerous non-autistic population, and thus language swiftly acquired a significant second root. This influence shows up most noticeably in the core vocabularies of the world's languages, dominated by words, phrases and metaphors derived out of the conditions of humanity's evolutionary, animal past. As the majority of humans were introduced to language, they adapted its content (autistic individuals might say they *corrupted* its content) to reflect those features of existence more natural and common to them— the businesses of eating, excreting, tribalizing, procreating. It is telling that it is *this* aspect of language that is most often accompanied by non-verbal cues and subtext.

In the early twenty-first century, human language stands as a well-mixed blend of its two sources of influence. The evolutionary, biological aspect of human language continues to hold prominence as its most frequently employed feature, from small talk to international diplomacy, and thus continues to serve its essential purpose of being the linguistic glue that helps hold the species together. But language's accelerating changes and additions, especially those introduced over the last several hundred years, reveal how the autistic root of human language has continued to become increasingly more influential, threatening to regain once more what might be described as its birthright. The periodic table, blueprints, box scores—one does not need to look far to recognize that the non-biological, non-evolutionary aspect of human language has been rapidly transforming the behavior of the human species and rapidly transforming the manner in which it communicates. And consider the education of children—the majority of whom pick up the core, biological aspects of language by the time they are five—but who require with each new generation more and more time, and a greater variety of instructional technique, to absorb just a fraction of the many new aspects of human language, absorb all the communicative structure being added with each passing year.

There is much we can learn about humanity simply by teasing from out of its language the various structures and contents, an analysis made most fruitful by recognizing that human language did not arise from a single source alone.

Two Sides of an Expressive Coin

Which came first for humans: language, or the awareness of temporal, spatial and other conceptual patterns?

Try imagining one without the other.

Derrida

But we had already seen this traveling medicine show! Hegel's puffoonery once pulled the wool over the eyes of an entire academic generation and sent countless grandstudents into a Rube Goldberg slumber. Note the reaction of both Schopenhauer and Kierkegaard—cogent, inspired, extraordinarily well written, as though the point to be demonstrated above all else is that when one has something worthy to say, one takes the trouble to say it well.

Universal Grammar

Although the term is correct, *universal grammar* has been given a meaning that does not match what those words actually say.

Noam Chomsky's early work in the field of linguistics deserves the highest praise. Before such efforts as *Syntactic Structures* (Chomsky 1957) and *Aspects of the Theory of Syntax* (Chomsky 1965), linguistics was stuck in a quagmire of piecemeal analysis—an irrelevant quicksand of phonemes, morphemes and dead-end semantics. Chomsky uncovered language's structural essence and promoted it to first-rate prominence, and his clever introduction of the tools of logic and recursive mathematics furnished linguistics with a language all its own, one that remains useful to the present day.

But Chomsky badly misguessed the *source* of language's structural underpinning, and in fact it is a bit of a puzzle why he had to make a guess at all. Having spent countless obsessive hours working through the many transformational rules of verbal syntax (his complete *The Logical Structure of Linguistic Theory* is so extensive it was only just recently made available in its entirety), Chomsky was given ample opportunity to recognize that his linguistic schemas had an immense amount in common with the formal rules of physics, mathematics, logic, chemistry, digital electronics and so many other non-biological disciplines. Space, time, proof, natural law, formal syntax—these concepts are in many ways so structurally similar they border on being isomorphic. So how could Chomsky have failed to recognize that as he was sketching out the structure of human language, he was also sketching out the basic structure of the experienced world? But such was the allure of brain science dogma even some forty odd years ago—Chomsky turned to biology instead and posited an instinct for human language.

To be fair, Chomsky was being handicapped by two critical pieces of evidence. One piece of evidence, in plain sight, proved to be an overly enticing red herring; and the other piece of evidence, far more useful and productive, was alas not available to Chomsky at all.

The red herring of course was the speed and apparent ease with which most children acquire spoken language. That an instinct was at the heart of this process was undeniable, but the first thing that should have been considered was whether an already known instinct could have adequately accounted for the phenomenon. The young of many species pass through a relatively brief period of rapid assimilation to their species' behaviors—learning to hunt, find shelter, meld to group social dynamics, and so forth—all leading quickly to adult-level skills in the areas of survival and procreation. The immense variety of these maturational activities makes it clear that it is not so much the activities themselves that are innate—what is instinctive in most animal species is their pedigree of being intensely *species aware* and *species imitative*.

Acute species recognition, to the degree of nearly complete perceptual exclusion of all other sensory input, is the common evolutionary thread that explains how the young of nearly every species rapidly transform into exact behavioral copies of all the other members of the population. Humans of course have been no different. When humans were once verbally silent hunter-gatherers, their children rapidly matured into being exact behavioral copies, taking on fully developed hunter-gatherer roles as early as the age of puberty. When humans then swiftly transformed into being both more verbal and more civilized, their children did not skip a maturational beat, just as quickly assuming this new set of common behaviors, brandishing them from a very early age. What most children have an instinct for is to do what other humans do. It has been that way for a very long time, and it still is.

But Chomsky became convinced that language had to be something different. With page after page of formulas and recursions laid out before him, aware more than anyone else of the complexity running throughout the entirety of syntax and semantics, Chomsky must have found it inconceivable that so much surface variation and core structural similarity could be acquired through species assimilation alone. In this, he was being hurt by his failure to see that it was not just language that was being newly absorbed by the human species, but also an entire assortment of corresponding behaviors and conventions, all with corresponding degrees of structural complexity. For Chomsky, language seemed to be something monolithic and thus became the sole focus of his attention, independent of these other new aspects of human behavior. Furthermore, language seemed to be something that had to be unique to this one species alone. Although hunting behaviors, sheltering behaviors, hierarchal behaviors—although these too are extraordinarily complex and their quick absorption no less amazing than the absorption of language, with thousands of other species able to serve for example and with the long reach of evolutionary time helping to soothe any concerns about how such behavioral complexity might be taken on, Chomsky did not doubt the species-assimilative forces when applied to such time-honored and widely distributed skills. Just not so language, the late-arriving skill without parallel. But even assuming Chomsky *could* have accepted that language might be absorbed by the usual species-assimilative means, this would have raised only a much larger question in his mind: where did language come from in the first place? Having appeared quite suddenly on this planet and having arrived as it were nearly full blown like Athena from Zeus's head, language would not have been able to chalk up its *origin* at the very least to some typical, down-through-the-generations event.

Faced with language's unique standing in the biological world and hampered by the seemingly unanswerable question regarding its origin, Chomsky resorted finally to some scientific magic and proposed an entirely separate instinct for human language. In one fell swoop Chomsky turned language into something biological, genetic, neural, evolutionary, and restrictively human. Thus the term *universal grammar* debuted as an ironic phrase, for now there was nothing universal in the concept at all.

The more productive piece of evidence that Chomsky did not have access to was an accurate description of the condition known as autism. Autism of course was known in the 1960s and 1970s, but at that time autism was regarded as little more than a medical catastrophe, its gravity compensated for only by its extreme rarity. The few autistic individuals who were recognized in Chomsky's day, both from the acuteness of their condition and from the cruelties likely being perpetrated upon them, would have been unable to provide many clues in a study of general linguistics. It would be at least another twenty years before the medical community would begin to recognize that autism was a condition not necessarily so devastating (and uncoincidentally, not all that uncommon), and of course even through the present day the medical community continues to struggle under the delusions from that misguided past.

Autism, when more accurately described, tells a much broader story than has been previously considered, a story touching upon, among many other things, the history and construction of human language.

Fundamentally, autistic individuals possess significantly less species recognition and species-assimilative capacity than do most other humans (and indeed, than do most other organisms). For reasons still unknown, autistic humans do not easily perceive human-specific features in their sensory environment, and therefore their initial sensory perception remains mostly ungrounded, with early autistic development running a gauntlet of a nearly overwhelming sensory chaos. In compensation and to varying degree, autistic individuals form their cognitive grounding instead out of the non-biological, structural features that inherently stand out from the surrounding environment—perceptions based primarily upon symmetry, patterns, repetition, order, and the like. The unusual early behaviors of autistic children are filled with the evidence from these unique forms of perception and cognition, with the developmental activities of nearly all autistic individuals—from childhood through maturity—showing marked preference for the more orderly, non-biological aspects of the objective world, rather than for the social, biologically-based features usually preferred by the human population at large.

Space, time, logic, mathematics—these concepts, representing the structural framework of the objective world, were introduced to the human species through the medium of autistic perception; they are the direct product of a compensatory form of autistic cognition that finds its essential grounding in the symmetries and patterns to be found in the surrounding world. Nonetheless, autistic individuals are biological creatures themselves and are therefore subject to the same set of restrictions on experience as are any other organism. Space, time, logic, mathematics—these concepts cannot be grasped by immediate biological perception alone, they are not an inherent part of immediate biological experience.

To bring non-biologically based perception into the realm of biological experience requires the aid of an intermediary. To bring non-biologically based perception into the realm of biological experience requires the use of an artifact that can be immediately and biologically perceived, but which also serves the purpose of representing that which is not biologically present. This intermediary is precisely that entity we call language, and if autistic individuals have been responsible for introducing the realm of non-biological pattern and structure to the human species, they have also been responsible for bringing along its essential companion—they have been responsible for the introduction of language.

If Chomsky had been able to contemplate an autism-inspired origin for human language, then perhaps he would have found himself less puzzled by the source and nature of language's underlying structure.

As the early artifacts of human language (abstract gestures to some degree but primarily spoken sounds) began to circulate around the globe, they quickly diverged both in vocabulary and surface form. But as Chomsky rightly noted, the underlying structure of human language changed hardly at all, never varied in any appreciable degree from tribe to tribe, from place to place, from generation to generation. This split between language's surface presentation and its underlying structure captures exactly the distinction between the *arbitrary nature of the artifacts doing the representing*, and the far more *determinant nature of the entity being represented*. Only the artifacts of language can be indeterminate, only they can take on a nearly unlimited guise—hundreds of spoken languages, thousands of individual dialects, written extensions, charts, symbols. As humans have so ably demonstrated, almost any sense-perceivable object can serve the purpose of conveying language; all that is required is some degree of convention. But although the artifacts of language can be derived from almost any perceivable source, what language *represents* is of a class entirely different. What language represents, by necessity and by the original purpose of language, is something already perceptually determined.

Space, time, logic, mathematics, pattern, symmetry—these concepts representing the form of the objective world are precisely those concepts that must be reflected inside language's foundational structure. Object and concept, noun and verb, temporal tenses, spatial adjectives, all manner of nuanced prepositional form—as autistics introduced to humanity the patterned structures from the surrounding world, they introduced also the conveying mechanism that by necessity had to assume that world's organizational form. Thus there is no need to posit a genetic or neural instinct to explain language's underlying structure; one need only look to the patterns and symmetries of the surrounding world and realize that language has no choice but to be their mirror. And one need not confine language to the human species alone; any life-form perceptually open to the non-biological patterns of the surrounding environment would by necessity find itself relying upon the conveying mechanism of a deeply structural language. Biologically speaking, no alternative exists.

And so indeed, human language is framed by a universal grammar—far more universal than Chomsky ever managed to conceive.

Meta-Language as a Misuse of the Tool

Since all occurrences of human language manifest as physically immediate artifacts (visible and tactile gestures, sound vibrations in the air, marks on a page, etc.), language itself can be recursively represented by further expression of language. Representing language is no different in kind than representing knives and rocks and stairs. But a complete doubling back of language upon itself, alluring like a forbidden fruit, is too often done without sensible purpose.

The normal purpose of language is to make use of a biologically immediate artifact to represent something not biologically immediate. But when language represents language, it becomes the use of a biologically immediate artifact to represent something *already* biologically immediate, and thus confusion easily abounds. Far too often, meta-language betrays a misuse—and a misunderstanding—of the tool.

The Printing Press and the Internet

Each quantum leap in language dissemination breaks the stranglehold of a fossilized institution—the Church formerly, academia now.

Medieval and *mediocrity* share a similar root.

The Two Forms of Human Logic

Humanity currently perceives its world with the aid of two distinct forms of logic.

One form of logic derives from the evolutionary inheritance of our animal past. Its goal is survival and procreation of the species, and its impact has been to conceptualize the sensory world into food, danger, sex, shelter, and so forth. Darwin's genius was to expose the structure underlying this biological logic and to demonstrate its influence as witnessed from without and as experienced from within. Non-autistic individuals are born naturally into this form of logic—it is the *other* form of logic they must learn to acquire.

The other form of logic has been extremely recent in its genesis. Its goal remains unclear, but its impact has been to conceptualize the sensory world into pattern, shape, space, time, and the like. The genius of the Greeks and the fruit of the Renaissance has been to expose the structure of this non-biological logic and to lay out its influence as witnessed from without and as experienced from within. Autistic individuals are born naturally into this form of logic—it is the *other* form of logic they must learn to acquire.

Neither form of logic by itself has transcendent power. But combined, they have rapidly transformed this species and its experienced world. Combined, they have transformed individuals.

The Simple Greeting Exchange

"How are you?"

"Fine, thank you."

The simple greeting exchange—which technically does not constitute a meaningful use of language—serves as fertile ground for understanding some fundamental differences between autistic and non-autistic perspectives, and also serves as an occasion for respecting and valuing those differences.

The simple greeting exchange, especially as practiced by non-autistic individuals, is the quintessence of biological immediacy. If the verbal aspect of the exchange can be said to be *about* anything, it is about what is already biologically present—two members of the species *Homo sapiens* interacting within the same time and space constraints as the conversation itself. That is why it can be said that technically speaking, the simple greeting exchange is not a meaningful use of language. Language is ordinarily the use of a biologically immediate artifact (spoken sounds, for instance) to represent something that is not biologically present (an event removed in space or time). In the simple greeting exchange, everything that needs to be conveyed is *already* present, so of what purpose is the language?

In the simple greeting exchange—with the exception of the words— everything is ancient and complex. Such exchanges have been taking place on this planet from almost the beginning of biology itself, and although each exchange happens in no more than an instant, each occurrence conveys a cornucopia of species-driven information forged from the long-burning furnace of evolutionary time. Observe two members of almost any animal species as they come together—ants along the trail, lions in their den, barracuda on the prowl—each exchange is just as eloquent, just as informational, as any end-of-the-month business transaction. In mammals, and in primates especially, this exchange is brought about by means of a precise set of sensory-based conventions—eye contact, body posture, clucks, coos, nuzzles, sniffs, licks, and so forth. Not a word ever needs to be spoken, and in all the other animal species, not a word *is* spoken. The other animal species have no conception of a yesterday or a tomorrow, no conception of a mile to the east or a mile to the west; so the other animal species have no need for language. And least of all do they have need for language during the simple greeting exchange—the epitome of conversational biological immediacy.

Humans were like this once too, and if we remove their words, we see that they still are.

Language was a late arrival on the human scene, and its purpose is far removed from being an aid to conversational biological immediacy. If the words of the simple greeting exchange can be said to have meaning beyond just their immediate occasion (an occasion that needs no words), it might be said that they serve as a marker, an indicator—they mark the occasion of a biologically immediate conversation. Humans, and in particular non-autistic humans, take the words of the simple greeting exchange as the signal that the intricate dance of eye contact, body posture and so on has begun. Or to give the notion more sophistication, humans might be said to be using the simple greeting exchange as an indicator that this is not an instance of biological immediacy *qua* animal, but instead an instance of biological immediacy in the context of greater civility. (But then again, each participant already knows that.)

In the simple greeting exchange, the text dissolves to nothing, and the subtext expands to incorporate everything.

Autistic individuals often find themselves discomfited by the simple greeting exchange. One of the reasons for this is that autistic individuals will sometimes take the simple greeting exchange quite literally—that is, they will take it as an expression of language. For instance, they understand "fine" to be an accurate report of the other person's status, only to discover that perhaps the circumstances were otherwise ("Couldn't you see the anger in my face?" the other will say). In response to "How are you?" or "What's been happening?", autistic individuals will often provide a detailed and factual account of their recent situation—spatially, temporally and logically arranged—and will find themselves bewildered when they realize the other person is bewildered by the reply.

Language, by its original intent, bridges the gap between biological immediacy and the more remote realms of space, time and non-biological structure and pattern. Autistic individuals intuitively understand this, because cognitively speaking, they exist far more comfortably within those more distant realms.

"How many ceiling fans do you have in your house?"

"What an interesting question! I have three ceiling fans in my house."

"What rooms are they in?"

"Let's see ... there is one in the living room, one in the bedroom, and another one on the porch."

"Is the ceiling fan on the porch spinning?"

The autistic greeting exchange is a work of art, although it is seldom recognized as such. It is a work of art primarily because it uses language almost exclusively in its original and creative form—as a biologically immediate artifact intended to represent, or to inquire about, an event spatially, temporally or biologically removed. When the autistic greeting exchange goes well, an autistic participant feels informed, and thus also feels comforted and welcomed—the same feelings a non-autistic individual receives upon a successful simple greeting exchange.

In the autistic greeting exchange, the text encompasses everything, and the subtext disappears.

Imagine a behavioral speech therapist trying to teach the simple greeting exchange to a young autistic child—employing countless discrete trials, wondering why progress is so painfully slow, perplexed by how the skill does not transfer outside the training room. But if the therapist were instead to teach the child the *autistic* greeting exchange—incorporating ceiling fans, light switches, Thomas the Tank Engine, or whatever else might be of interest to this particular child—would not the child's attention perk up almost immediately? Would not progress be considerably faster and the skills more widely acquired? "But that's not the goal," the therapist will object. "The goal is not to have the child greet people with inappropriate banter about ceiling fans, light switches or Thomas the Tank Engine. The goal is to have the child greet people with the simple greeting exchange."

Inappropriate is indeed the correct adjective here, but not applied to the banter. Is the aim of this therapy to teach the child the use of language, or to make the child indistinguishable from all his peers?

Autistic individuals will often bemoan the pettiness and insincerity of the simple greeting exchange, but that is a misunderstanding—they are overlooking billions of years of intricate and essential biology.

Non-autistic individuals will often decry the inappropriateness of the autistic greeting exchange, but that is also a misunderstanding—they are overlooking the origin, and the glory, of a creative use of words.

Logic for Autistics

As a subject of investigation, logic has undergone a surge in development over the past one hundred fifty years, resulting in enhanced clarification of the topic and a wider application to much of human endeavor. Iconic names such as Boole, Peirce, Frege, Russell, Wittgenstein, Tarski and Gödel all have contributed groundbreaking insights, their advancements leading not only to transformations within the field of logic itself, but spawning also concomitant reappraisals in such areas as mathematics, science and linguistics. This past century and a half has seen logic's golden era,

Yet for all that, critical questions remain unresolved at logic's core. To put it bluntly, we still have not found an effective way to describe *fundamentally* what gives rise to logical properties, and perhaps just as importantly, we have yet to uncover a plausible explanation for how logic must have originated in man. How is it that humanity has come to possess logical abilities, given that the other animal species display no evidence of possessing similar abilities, and given that the arrival of these characteristics in man—at least their *effective* arrival—seems to have occurred only quite recently in the species' history?

These questions regarding logic's elemental traits have been pondered by a variety of logicians and philosophers, but in truth only a few have attempted to tackle the problem head on, and only one, Wittgenstein, has danced daringly close to an accurate answer. There is good reason these questions have remained unresolved. In retrospect, we are beginning to realize logicians and philosophers have been hampered in their efforts to understand logic's nature because they have been missing a vital piece of information, and without that piece of information they have been making the tacit assumption that logic must have arisen from an *homogeneous* form of human perception and cognition. It is only in the last few decades that humanity has begun to realize this tacit assumption is not altogether accurate and has begun to recognize within itself the condition that stands as the key to unlocking logic's core, a condition that reveals, most crucially, the nature of humanity's surprising cognitive composition.

In this essay I will attempt to shed light on the nature of logic's most fundamental characteristics, and I will offer an answer to the question of how logic first originated in man. I will address these matters not so much logically and philosophically as I will describe them biologically and anthropologically; for in short, it is *autism* that stands as the key to understanding logic. The thesis of this essay is that logic's fundamental characteristics are generated naturally and spontaneously out of the biological circumstances of autistic perception.

History. In the Western tradition, logic was dominated for more than two millennia by Aristotle's *Organon* and its emphasis on syllogistic reasoning. The *Organon* sounds surprisingly modern given its age of origin, but it also lacks enough expressive power to represent the full range of human cognition and inference, and thus in the mid-nineteenth century a revolution began that would quickly overthrow syllogistic logic's enduring reign.

The first stirrings of this revolution can be seen in the work of George Boole, who in likening his laws of thought to the operations of mathematics began a process of treating logic as a type of calculus, one best represented and best manipulated under the guise of a formal symbolism. Shortly thereafter and independently of each other, Charles Sanders Peirce in the United States and Gottlob Frege in Germany introduced several techniques that greatly expanded logic's expressive range—the use of quantifiers, a greater emphasis on relations, and a rigorous employment of functions and variables to illuminate the role of various logical elements. By the time such techniques were gathered under the compilative work of Bertrand Russell, who himself would add important insights on the process of denoting, logic had gained enough expressive power to state precisely nearly all the meaningful assertions that could be made under the headings of inference, mathematics and objective science, and it was upon this foundation that twentieth-century logicians Alfred Tarski and Kurt Gödel applied logical technique to logic itself (metalogic) and developed surprising and paradoxical results regarding the power and range of any deductive calculus. Riding the crest of these many developments, modern logic would blossom by the end of the twentieth century (blossom too much, some might say) into a multi-faceted academic industry.

As can be gathered from the above description, the majority of logic's recent developments have had the effect of changing the manner in which logic is *done*, but occasionally there have been logicians who have also paused to ask more fundamental questions, in particular to ask what exactly do these new logical developments *mean*, how are they to be related to human cognition and to the qualities of the experienced world. Gottlob Frege, for instance, frequently pondered the philosophical context of his logical and mathematical innovations, and in such classic works as *Concept and Object*, *On Sense and Reference*, and *Thought: A Logical Investigation*, Frege brought new perspectives to bear upon the notions of meaning, sense, language, object, concept, truth and world. One unusual and highly suggestive aspect of Frege's philosophy is the degree to which he strives ruthlessly to *objectify* his particular brand of logic. In positing True and False as actual objects of the external world, and in insisting again and again that non-scientific accounts (the stories of the *Odyssey*, for instance) possess sense but no actual reference, Frege appears to be making a determined effort to banish everything subjective from the privileged domains of logic, mathematics and scientific discourse, and one is left with the distinct impression that Frege's ultimate goal was to purify logic of every last ounce of human influence, as though such influence could serve only to mess things up.

Frege, along with Bertrand Russell, also had the noteworthy impact of inspiring and encouraging a young Ludwig Wittgenstein. Wittgenstein differs markedly from the other figures in logic's recent history in that he was never interested in *developing* logic so much as he was driven to describe it and to explain its role (its *office*, as he was inclined to say). And in a type of subconscious loyalty to his principle regarding the need to show instead of say, Wittgenstein throughout his far-ranging, sometimes fast-changing philosophical career seems to have *embodied* his most valuable logical insights as much as he managed to state them.

Wittgenstein's early philosophy, crystallized in the *Tractatus Logico-Philosophicus*, takes as its starting point the logical framework of Frege and Russell, but quickly adds to that framework an orthogonal extension designed to highlight logic's connection to experience, language and the world. And in a surprising twist that would have dismayed Frege (assuming Frege could have understood it), Wittgenstein takes the notion of objectifying logic, of purifying it of all human influence, and turns that notion completely on its head. In the *Tractatus*, Wittgenstein seems to be employing the tools of logic to construct a type of near solipsism, an inspired attempt as it were to animate Kierkegaard's cry of "truth is subjectivity" by outlining it with step-by-step instructions. On its surface, the *Tractatus* still sounds objective and logical, but viewed from within it reads as extraordinarily self-generated—Wittgenstein's startling depiction of the world as he found it, an embodiment of his both unique and universal form of perception.

Although Wittgenstein was initially convinced the *Tractatus* contained unassailable truth, he grew nonetheless ever more restless with its emphasis on formal logic, and upon returning to philosophy more than a decade after having finished the *Tractatus*, Wittgenstein began re-examining logic from an entirely different angle. This so-called later philosophy, gathered primarily in the posthumously published *Philosophical Investigations*, examines the structure and meaning of *ordinary* language, and emphasizes not only the role of propositional assertions, but also that of questions, commands and sudden exclamations. Wittgenstein begins to explore the impact of community and what he calls "forms of life" as he attempts to describe the communal scaffolding whereby structure and meaning are shared, and in contrast to both Frege's strident objectivity and the *Tractatus*' strident subjectivity, Wittgenstein's later philosophy takes on the style and form of a mutual investigation, an investigation dealing in many ways with the natural history of man.

Academicians like to emphasize the break between Wittgenstein's early and late philosophies, but it should be noted that Wittgenstein's later work does not so much *abandon* the logic of the *Tractatus* as it attempts to *supplement* it. For a period of time Wittgenstein seriously contemplated a project in which the *Tractatus* would be published side-by-side with his new remarks, each text shedding light and contrast upon the other. Such a side-by-side project would have been visually significant for Wittgenstein, for it would have laid out structurally the nature of the problem most vexing him. Like nearly all philosophers before him, Wittgenstein had assumed the traits of human logic flowed from a common well, and yet here he had been developing a lifetime of philosophical work—as sincerely as any philosopher ever could—that presented two extremely *different* aspects of human logic, each of which appeared to be valuable and viable, but each of which appeared to be irreconcilable. Thus it would have been difficult for Wittgenstein to recognize how his two philosophies, embracing and embodying two different aspects of human logic, had managed in a certain sense to unveil logic's mysteries as accurately as anyone ever had, for it would have been difficult for him to reconcile logic's dual characteristic to just a single source.

Wittgenstein of course lived well before the condition of autism became widely known and more completely described. If Wittgenstein *had* known about autism, if he had been given a thorough description of autism's distinctive form of perception, I am certain he would have recognized almost immediately autism's direct bearing on his dual presentation of logic. Wittgenstein, as much as anyone, would have been able to recognize that here was an actual cause—not a philosophical or logical *reason*, but instead an actual biological and anthropological *cause*—for the two differing aspects of logic, aspects that as it turns out indeed warrant presentation side-by-side. With an accurate understanding of autism, we can see that the two aspects of logic have in fact two very real sources, sources emanating from the non-homogeneous composition of human cognition. And it is the first aspect of logic—the aspect Frege had tried to purify of human influence, the aspect Wittgenstein had employed in the *Tractatus* to construct his near solipsism, the aspect generally grouped by logicians under the heading of formal logic—it is that aspect of logic that arises naturally and spontaneously from the conditions of autistic perception.

Description. Autistic perception differs fundamentally from non-autistic perception.

The main characteristic of biological perception is its providing of a sensory foreground. Without foregrounding, each organism's broad array of sensory input would be experienced as undifferentiated and chaotic, and therefore it is critical that each organism be able to perceive some type of signal against its background of sensory noise. In the animal kingdom—and this would include man and his long history as a simple primate—evolution has forged a type of biological perception extremely well suited for survival and procreation, a type of perception best described by adjectives such as *species-specific* or *species-focused*. Each species member is born with a natural and spontaneous ability to focus primarily, if not exclusively, on the other members of the species and on the species' general interests and pursuits, and this ability allows each member to rapidly imitate the others and to assimilate to the species' overall behavior. This form of focused perception is of course extremely valuable; it allows each population to coalesce around its own members and around its sources of shelter and food, and thus species-specific perception contributes in a fundamental way to the quest for viability. But it should also be noted that this form of perception is so powerful it blocks alternative forms of perception, and thus has the effect of locking each species into a tight biological immediacy. Nowhere in the natural world do we find evidence of comprehensive, detailed perceptions centered on, for instance, the shapes of geography, the cycles of botany, the patterns of weather, or the course of the celestial seasons. Nowhere in the natural world do these items ever manage to achieve perceptual foregrounding.

Although something has clearly changed *man's* perceptual capacity—broadening it remarkably in a very short period of time—for the large majority of humans, their natural and spontaneous form of biological perception can still be described unambiguously as being *species-specific*. The early attentive focus of most children continues to gravitate to sensory impressions made upon them by other humans and by the population's behaviors and interests, and as happened not that long ago on prehistoric African plains, children today employ a species-specific perception to rapidly imitate the others and to assimilate to the population's current behaviors. And despite mankind's unprecedented departure from circumstances once fraught with the struggles of survival and procreation, humans today continue to display foremost interest in the biological concerns of species—sex, family, food, shelter, societal ranking. Man has remained for the most part a social and biological being, he has carried his evolutionary inheritance of a species-specific focus right with him into modern times, and it is these strong, lingering, *foregrounding* traits of a species-specific focus that define the distinguishing characteristics of typical non-autistic perception.

Autistic perception differs fundamentally from non-autistic perception in that autistic perception, to a significant degree, lacks this species-specific focus. The material cause for this difference remains unknown (a variety of genetic, neurological and biochemical hypotheses have been proposed, but so far none have proven enlightening); the characteristics of this difference, however, are apparent from observation alone. Observation consistently reveals that autistic individuals display considerably less perceptual preference for humans and human biological influences, and show much greater perceptual attention for an entirely different class of sensory features.

Recall that the main task of biological perception is to provide sensory foregrounding. If autistic individuals are not experiencing a natural and spontaneous foregrounding of human-specific features from their surrounding environment, then the question arises, what *does* foreground for them, if anything at all? Autistic individuals would appear to be at risk of large-scale sensory chaos and confusion, and there is some evidence that such a potential does exist, for many autistic individuals do report a variety of sensory difficulties that do not derive from any known physical cause. In general, however, autistic individuals do not experience complete sensory chaos and confusion; certain features from their surrounding environment do consistently foreground and emerge. These features possess the particular trait of being able to inherently stand out, they form an implicit signal against a background of sensory noise, and these features are what humans now categorize under the headings of symmetry, repetition, pattern, structure, mappings and the like. Unfettered by the strong species-specific focus characteristic of non-autistic perception, and in need of sensory foregrounding to avoid complete sensory confusion, autistic individuals are drawn to those elements from the broadly arrayed environment that inherently emerge from the background, elements rich in pattern, structure and form. It is this natural and spontaneous foregrounding of structural, mostly non-biological features from the surrounding environment that defines the distinguishing characteristic of autistic perception.

And here is the direct connection to formal logic: *this basic process of implicit sensory foregrounding experienced within autistic perception corresponds exactly to the foundational components of formal logic.*

The foundational components of formal logic can be classified in various ways—different logicians will use slightly different approaches—but almost any classification will include a detailed description of the following three core features of logic:

- Objects
- Concepts
- Relations

These three core features of logic are in a certain sense indefinable, but it is possible to cast greater light upon their nature and upon their likely human origin by realizing that each core feature corresponds to an aspect of foregrounding within autistic perception. Each core feature of logic corresponds to a particular type of implicit perceptual emergence from a background of sensory noise.

The notion *object* plays a role in all three core features of logic, but as a standalone target of investigation, *object* is probably best approached through the idea of an unanalyzable entity, an entity highlighted most often within formal logic through the use of a proper name. It would be difficult to suggest a notion more basic than that of *object*.

If we begin with an image of undifferentiated biological perception (a sensory chaos, if you will) and envision the spontaneous emergence of a single, unanalyzable entity from within that perception, then we will have a rough model for the type of perceptual foregrounding that gives rise to the notion *object*. For non-autistic individuals, their natural inclination is to have other *humans* be the entities which foreground within their perception (and of course the naming of people has become an essential part of human discourse). But for autistic individuals, their basic experience of perceptual foregrounding by necessity must be more generic, and in consequence produces a more generalized paradigm for the notion *object*. Since autistic individuals lack in significant degree the ability to foreground human features from their surrounding environment, it becomes incumbent upon the sensory field itself to provide the characteristics that can implicitly emerge in autistic perception, and from the experience of autistic individuals, we know that such implicit emergence is provided most often by entities that embody such attributes as symmetry, repetition and pattern. The classic example from autistic experience would be the strong perceptual attraction of spinning objects—tops, wheels, ceiling fans. A spinning object strongly embodies visual symmetry and patterned repetition, and in an otherwise undifferentiated sensory environment, items such as ceiling fans would inherently stand out; they are more easily (more naturally, more spontaneously) foregrounded against a background of sensory noise.

This description of the notion *object* is distinctive, because here, it is the entity itself which embodies the structural or patterned characteristic, and thus it is the entity itself which carries the impetus for its implicit foregrounding. As we will discover momentarily, objects encountered under the notions *concept* and *relation* are in a certain sense less distinctive, and thus are treated in formal logic more anonymously. But as a first step it is important to consider separately, as we have here, this more distinctive version of the notion *object*, because its extremely simple and self-contained nature is highly suggestive of the more basic aspects of formal logic. For instance, the foregrounding/ non-foregrounding dichotomy contained in the notion *object* hints at the binary nature underlying much of logic, including the binary nature of *true* and *false*. Furthermore, the unique accompaniment of such non-biological attributes as symmetry, repetition and pattern highlights the atypical nature of *object* as experienced within autistic perception, and thus points to that perception as the likely source for mankind's cognitive separation from the remainder of the animal kingdom. Just as importantly, the solitary distinctiveness of the notion *object*, its unencumbered simplicity during sensory emergence, provides perhaps the most basic example available of the direct linkage between the characteristics of biological perception and the nature of human logic.

With the notion *concept*, unlike with the notion *object*, it is not the entity itself which embodies the structural or patterned characteristic; instead, with *concept*, it is more commonly the case that objects *constitute* the structural or patterned characteristic, and it is the characteristic itself, often abstract, that gives rise to the notion *concept*. Classic examples from autistic experience would include the lining up of toys or the rapt attention paid to a series of sounds produced in repeated temporal pattern (evenly spaced claps, for instance). Note that each object by itself (each toy, each clap) would not tend to foreground within autistic perception, because each object by itself does not embody the structural characteristic necessary for it to be perceived against a background of sensory noise. Instead it is the formed *concept* (the straight line, the rhythm) which carries the symmetrical or patterned trait that allows it to implicitly emerge within autistic perception, and the constituting objects in a certain sense merely come along for the perceptual ride. It is the foregrounding of such structural and often abstract features that lies at the heart of the notion *concept*.

In formal logic, the notion *concept* was clarified greatly by the developments of the late nineteenth century, in particular by the introductions put forth by Frege. In adding quantifiers, variables and functions to the discourse and philosophy behind formal logic, Frege helped capture more precisely the essence of the notion *concept*. For example, in the use of a first-order logical formula such as "For all x: f(x)," it becomes apparent that it is the concrete objects that are being treated iteratively and anonymously, while it is the function itself, representing the *concept*, that carries all the distinctiveness of the statement. That is to say, it is the concept-representing function that *foregrounds* in such statements of formal logic, and such functional foregrounding reflects precisely the foregrounding of *concepts* within biological perception.

Furthermore, it would appear that the genesis of the notion *concept* must be particularly autistic, for nowhere else in the animal kingdom is there evidence of perceptual awareness directed towards structural, abstract *concepts*, and neither is there evidence of such awareness in the early history of man. To contemplate a purely *non-autistic* version of the notion *concept*, we would need to consider the perceptual emergence of similar, but more *biologically*-derived features, and although such features are certainly thinkable and likely, these are features that nonetheless would be quite different in kind from the usual notion *concept*. Thus the sudden expansion of human perceptive range, including its impact upon the recent transformations in the culture of man, must be attributed in large measure to the introduction of abstract patterns and symmetries— the material of the notion *concept*—an introduction achieved primarily through the implicit, mostly non-biological foregrounding necessitated by the circumstances of autistic perception.

Relations, like *concepts*, are also constituted out of objects, but here what gives rise to perceptual foregrounding is not that the objects form into a particular pattern or structure, but that the objects consistently *map* to one another (in fact under many scenarios, such as those involving language, *mapping* would make a much better term than *relation*). If we start again with an image of undifferentiated biological perception, we can now focus on those examples where two or more objects consistently co-occur within the sensory field—for instance, two flashes of light that always happen simultaneously, or one flash of light that always takes place at the same time as a particular sound. Each flash and each sound by itself would not emerge in autistic perception, not without embodying some structural feature (as with distinctive *objects*), and the *collection* of flashes and sounds also cannot emerge in autistic perception, not unless that collection happens to constitute a discernible pattern (as with *concepts*). But the consistent *mapping* is enough all by itself, it is all that is required to break the background chaos and provide a means whereby to gain sensory foregrounding. It is when the consistent co-occurrence of two or more objects in the sensory field gains perceptual attention that we have a well-formed instance of the notion *relation*.

Relations have two important consequences. As suggested by the example of a light flash mapping to a particular sound, *relations* can arise from objects that map across sensory domains, and thus *relations* provide a useful framework for sensory integration in autistic perception. Note that non-autistic individuals already have a built-in framework for sensory integration; their focused perception on human-specific features provides a natural touch point for gathering experiences of sight, sound, touch, smell and even taste. But autistic individuals, without a similar perceptual focus, and with their experiences of *objects* and *concepts* frequently taking place in only a single sensory domain, find themselves in need of a perceptual mechanism that can tie together sensory experience, and the cross-domain potential of *relations* fits that need quite nicely. The other important consequence of *relations* is that they provide a paradigm for the creation of language. Language is a higher-level construct than the notion *relation*, but language follows a similar outline, for language is essentially a mapping, a mapping from biologically immediate artifacts onto entities and concepts not so biologically present. And as *relations* serve an integrative purpose in autistic perception, so too does language serve an integrative purpose across the entire human species. In the first place, language pulls together the expanded cognitive experience brought on by awareness of *objects*, *concepts* and *relations*, and furthermore language brings together the differing aspects of autistic and non-autistic perception, serving as the medium in which to blend autistic and non-autistic cognitive traits, thereby fostering a perceptual transformation in all mankind.

The remainder of formal logic is built up largely out of these three core features of logic—that is, the more complex logical components, such as propositions, logical product, logical sum, and so on, these are generally constructed out of various combinations of *objects*, *concepts* and *relations*. And from the perspective of autistic perception, this climb from simplicity through constructed complexity mirrors the developmental climb from childhood through maturity. Autistic sensory foregrounding tends to become ever more sophisticated as basic perceptions, apprehended concurrently, are built into more complex perceptions based upon the emergence of the many permutations. Wittgenstein's *Tractatus* in fact unfolds in much this same manner, building up its version of logic out of *objects* and states of affairs (*concepts* and *relations*), combining these into propositions of limitless constructibility, and then by extension building up similar frameworks to describe the development of world and self. In the *Tractatus*, perhaps as no place else, we find constructive logic, developing autistic perception, and the author's own maturing self all being brought together into one tightly organized, self-presenting mirror.

To be as precise as possible, in this discussion outlining the anthropological origin of the core features of logic, it is only the process of *perceptual foregrounding* that directly corresponds to the topic of logic. The characteristics of the features that actually foreground— that is, the characteristics of structure, symmetry, pattern, and the like—these characteristics belong, technically speaking, to a different topic; they belong to mathematics. Visual symmetry and structure for instance make up the core material of geometry, and the various types of repetition and pattern, these form the basis of arithmetic. As such, it is interesting to recall the Logicism projects of both Frege and Russell, who attempted to construct the entirety of mathematics upon a foundation of formal logic, efforts ultimately dispelled by Gödel's incompleteness theorem. From the perspective of autistic perceptual foregrounding, we can see perhaps yet another reason why Logicism cannot entirely succeed, because within the perceptual foregrounding process the characteristics of logic and mathematics reveal themselves as essentially inseparable—they are much like two sides of one coin. The foregrounding process itself (logic) would not be possible if it were not for the structural features in the sensory environment (mathematics) that could inherently emerge; and on the other hand, from the lack of mathematical awareness in the animal kingdom we know that the environment's non-biological, structural features would remain entirely unapprehended if it were not for the presence of an unfettered form of perception in which such features could take preeminent place. Logic and mathematics are intricately intertwined, it would appear to be hopeless to build either out of the other. Furthermore, we may as well add objective science into this same mix of inseparability; for with geometry being the basis of space, and with arithmetic being the basis of time, and with logical inference being the basis of scientific method, science's entire *modus operandi* traces directly back to the characteristics of logic and mathematics, and therefore traces directly back to the characteristics of autistic perception. In a fundamental sense (and in a biological and anthropological sense), the characteristics of logic, mathematics and science form an uncleavable whole.

It should also be noted that if foregrounding within autistic perception is to be identified as a logic—in this case, formal logic—then foregrounding within *non-autistic* perception must be identified as a logic as well. Humans have yet to develop a precise language for depicting this more species-specific version of perceptual foregrounding—although its characteristics can be hinted at through the terminology of Darwinian and sociological principles, such terminology often remains too murky. It would be of immense value, however, to develop a more precise language for depicting species-focused forms of logic, for with such a language, alongside the language of formal logic, researchers could more accurately compare and contrast autistic and non-autistic perceptual characteristics, and nowhere would that precise investigation be more informative than in the area of linguistics.

Linguistics—the study of the logic behind human language— encompasses much too large a topic to be taken up here, but a general approach emerges quite naturally as an extension to the investigation of formal logic (thereby traveling much the same road as Wittgenstein did proceeding from the *Tractatus* to the *Philosophical Investigations*).

One critical aspect of this approach is to realize that ordinary human language cannot be analyzed accurately without recognizing that human language derives historically and anthropologically out of *both* forms of human logic. The formal logic that arises from autistic perception provides the impetus and much of the underlying structure for human language, while the biological, species-specific logic that is the birthright of non-autistic perception provides a substantial and significant addendum, one that above all else helps to disseminate language across the entirety of the human species. Until we recognize and emphasize these dual roots of a now thoroughly blended human language, we will continue to find linguistics a most puzzling subject—puzzling with respect to language's content, structure and origin. As an example, see Chapter 2, Section 2.3, of *Aspects of the Theory of Syntax* (Chomsky 1965) and the "problem" described therein. Much of this so-called problem can be traced to the dual logical roots of human language, and although Chomsky's solution of dividing linguistic processing into a base phrase grammar—incorporating much of formal logic—and a separate supplemental lexicon—incorporating much of species-specific logic—although this solution points to the dual aspect and dual origin of human language, Chomsky and his followers have never seemed to recognize this possibility for what it actually is.

Two Concluding Observations. An observation to make regarding the history of modern logic is that nearly all its significant contributors have been individuals who have displayed behaviors and interests consistent with those of an autistic personality. With the possible exception of Tarski (who although atypical in many respects, was clearly the most outgoing and collaborative of the group), modern logic was developed almost entirely by men who tended towards introversion, eccentricity and obsession, men whose biographies are filled with a clear preference for facts, objects and rules, and a clear discomfort with people, society and the demands of human convention. The autistic characteristics of Frege and Wittgenstein, for instance, seem nearly indisputable, and yet even those two examples would have to be described as relatively mild compared to the more extreme cases of Peirce and Gödel, each of whom displayed eccentricities that might easily be interpreted as pathological.

There is nothing coincidental about this observation. The fields of logic, mathematics and science have *always* been saturated with personalities possessing autistic-like characteristics, a fact made more prominent when focusing on those individuals who have made the most significant and transformational contributions. Autistic individuals are *drawn* to such disciplines, they display a preternatural ability to be creative in such domains. The characteristics of logic, mathematics and science reflect exactly—indeed, were originated out of—the basic conditions of autistic perception. And it should be noted how recent and sudden has been the appearance of these disciplines within the culture of man; there is little, if any, evidence of their existence in mankind's more animal-like past. Thus the rise of logic, mathematics and science cannot be described as an evolutionary event, but instead mirrors the rise of these disciplines' more proximate cause, mirrors the increasing presence and significance of autistic cognitive traits within the human population.

An observation to make regarding this essay's basic description of formal logic—as the process of inherent, non-biological foregrounding emerging from an autistic individual's background of sensory noise—is how closely this description matches the spontaneous activities of young autistic children. There exist many studies now that demonstrate autistic children's preference for perceptions and activities rich in non-biological pattern and structure over the perceptions and activities heavily influenced by social or biological form. And in a more informal sense, the many commonly reported behaviors of autistic children—lining up toys, spinning wheels and tops and selves, fascination with digits and letters, listening to the same song over and over, watching the same video again and again—these activities reveal the nearly compulsive manner in which young autistic children focus primarily on the features of non-biological pattern and structure to be found in the world around them, exactly as this essay's description of logic and autistic perception would directly predict.

That autism researchers have been unable to make this observation themselves is indeed one of modern science's greatest travesties, for it derives from autism scientists not trying to *understand* autistic behaviors so much as they have been trying to *destroy* them. Drugs, behavioral therapies, other atrocities that go under the heading of *early intervention*—these have fast become the sole scientific means by which autism researchers now investigate the activities of young autistic children. Thus autism scientists remain entirely blind to the rich information these children have to impart.

This travesty must end.

If humanity's goal is to understand more fully the foundations and origins of its logical thinking, if humanity's desire is to describe more accurately man's sudden transformation from animal into logical being, then humanity must end this all-too-common practice of brutally misunderstanding the key to its most vital logical questions. Humanity must end this all-too-common practice of brutally misunderstanding its autistic individuals.

The Attack
on Sciencedom

Shock and Awe

It might seem like ancient history to those who are jostling shoulders in the laboratory halls, but it was not that long ago—not even a third of Kierkegaard's eighteen hundred years—that science was the province of the near lunatic only, that rare soul born so lonely into his experienced world he could not help but be drawn to its beckoning call. And although even in those former times there were many well-established, codified, standardized means for exploring one's experienced world— for instance, one could pray to God and wait for helpful reply—such techniques tended to require infinite patience, and alas, near lunatics are not known for their infinite patience. Thus it was that a few of these miscreant souls began taking matters into their own hands, and how was humanity to have known, there on its knees before God, that the world would not be averse to divulging its dazzlements and amazements directly, even by unapproved, nonstandard means.

How much of that iconoclastic spirit remains alive today? Well, ask the tens of millions of scientists who now live and work among us, but while you are asking, notice how undazzled and how unamazed they all appear to be. Peer review and standards. Funding and credentials. Mind-numbing technique. What science has become—in less than a third of Kierkegaard's eighteen hundred years—is little more than a warm and safe profession, the methodologized, codified road map that runs cowering from shock and awe. As far as modern science is concerned, we may as well return to praying to God.

Good Science

If science is merely a methodology, then in the current era it has become the preferred method of minutiae and mediocrity.

Think about it. We now live among literally millions and millions of scientists, the large majority of whom practice, in the well-intended words of Ben Goldacre, good science (Goldacre 2008). They dutifully form their hypotheses, they dutifully conduct their experiments, and they dutifully record all their critical data. And when the harvesting time of publication comes around (and when the services of enough well-connected co-authors have been dutifully gathered), these good scientists patiently submit their findings to peer review and wait longingly for reply. In the thousands and thousands of unread journals now clogging our crowded shelves we might find the outpourings of these good scientists' many tireless efforts—detailed insights into fatherless mice, dark halo density profiles, dysfunctional amygdalas, and the priming effects of macrophages. If good science is a blessing, then our cup truly runneth over.

But where, might I ask, is the brilliant science? Where might I find that scientist equivalent to a Newton, a Darwin, an Einstein—each of whom appeared to be far less concerned with following the prescribed recipes of good science than with turning good science upon its head? With millions and millions of good scientists now rubbing their shoulders against us, why is the brilliant science not more abundantly ripe for the picking, and why do we assume this dearth of brilliant science is in no way connected to the massive proliferation of good science?

I will say it again: if science is merely a methodology, then in the current era it has become the preferred method of minutiae and mediocrity.

Limbo Dancing

Publication—the new standard of scientific evidence.
Statistics software—the new standard of scientific effort.
Postdoctoral fellowship—the new standard of scientific courage.
Citation—the new standard of scientific community.
Peer review—the new standard of critical thinking.
Questionnaire—the new standard of scientific measurement.
Experimental design—the new standard of scientific insight.
Co-authors—the new standard of reproducibility.
Grant proposal—the new standard of scientific innovation.
Grant approval—the new standard of scientific achievement.
Good science—the new standard.

Three Questions Poorly Asked

What aspect of brain neurology gives rise to human intelligence and reasoning?

What evolutionary mechanism underlies the ascent of human culture and civilization?

What etiology explains the disorder known as autism?

They say that a question well asked is a question already half answered: the examples above show that a question poorly asked cannot be answered at all.

The Futility of More and More Studies

Everywhere in the autism research community can be heard the cry for more and more studies. More trials, more equipment, more subjects, more data, more funding. The phrase "further research is needed in this area" has become so hackneyed within autism science it deserves its own special symbol (might I suggest the emoticon of an outstretched palm).

Listen, I like data as much as the next guy, but lack of data is not the problem in autism research. We have a mountain of data already, with more truckloads arriving daily. We are practically buried under autism research data.

The problem is not lack of data. The problem is lack of vision.

The Massive Hunt

As we approach an ever more accurate assessment of autism's prevalence within the human population, the cry grows ever more shrill to identify autism's environmental cause. Never mind that we have been searching diligently for that cause for more than a decade now and have yet to find its first trace. Never mind all that, because autism has unquestionably reached an epidemic stage, and with autism such a devastating illness, especially untreated, we could not possibly have overlooked its debilitating consequences in all the years before (and no, there is no need to question such obvious assumptions). Look harder, look faster: autism's environmental cause *has* to be there.

In the late nineteenth century, scientists embarked on a massive hunt for the luminiferous ether. Never mind that they had been searching diligently for the ether for quite some time and had yet to find its first trace. Never mind all that, because light's properties were unquestionably those of waves, and with the characteristics of space, time and energy so well understood, the absence of a propagating medium was something quite unthinkable (and no, there was no need to question such obvious assumptions). The scientists looked harder, looked faster: the luminiferous ether *had* to be there.

Pharmacology

Here is a list of medications commonly used in the treatment of autism: Prozac, Risperdal, Adderall, Depakote, Zoloft, Tegretol, Mellaril, Lithobid, Wellbutrin, Haldol, Zyprexa, Anafranil, Ritalin.

But exactly what problem are we solving here?

If I were to say I was interested in playing sports, and then donned simultaneously a goalie's mask, sweat pants, shin pads, boxing gloves, wrist band, snow skis, shoulder pads, racing silks, swimming goggles and a catcher's mitt, would you not think I had gone slightly mad? At the very least, would you not think I had misunderstood the phrase "playing sports"?

There is no "treatment of autism" in that list of drugs. And yes, we have gone slightly mad.

Snapshot

Someone needs to perform an fMRI study on personal computers—say, Intel-based machines versus some Macs. Each comparison group can be resonance photographed while performing the same task, for instance the monthly payroll. I suspect there will be some differences.

Since the Intel-based machines are in more widespread use, their images can be presumed to be the healthy ones, with the areas of highest concentrated glow described as the likely location for a monthly payroll module (greatly advancing our understanding of that mysterious concept called accounting). In contrast, the electronic flows of the Macs can be described as disordered and dysfunctional, with various treatment options—such as battery boost, a well-placed bobby pin, or just a good kick—being offered for consideration.

What today's brain imaging studies show most clearly is our own muddled thinking.

Genetic Litany

Chromosome 7q36, engrailed homeobox 2(EN2), the 16p11.2 region, 15q11.2, 15q13.3, 16p13.11; four regions located on 18q (MBD1, TCF4, NETO1, FBXO15); the PON1 gene; MECP2, TM4SF2, TSPAN7, PPP1R3F, PSMD10, MCF2, SLITRK2, GPRASP2, and OPHN1; encoding methyl CpG-binding protein 2; the SHANK2 synaptic scaffolding gene; the 5-HT(2A) receptor gene; neurexin-1 (NRXN1), chromosome 17p13.3, the two genes TUSC5 and YWHAE.

Cell adhesion molecule 1 (CADM1); RELN and GRIK2; MKL2 and SND1; chromosome Xp22.11-p21.2 that encompasses the IL1RAPL1 gene; the GABA receptor gamma 3 (GABRG3); neuroligin (NLGN4X); the FMR1 gene; region 10p14-p15, 7p22.1, the Q6NUR6 gene, JMJD2C gene at 9p24.1, 1p21.1, 6p21.3 and 8q21.13; Mecp2-null microglia; R1117X and R536W; SHANK3 mutations, GABA(A) receptor subunits, ASMT, MTNR1A, MTNR1B; RORA and BCL-2 proteins; DOCK4 microdeletion on 7q31.1, 2q14.3 microdeletion disrupting CNTNAP5; chromosome 2q24.2—>q24.3, telencephalic GABAergic neurons, position 614 of diaphanous homolog 3 (DIAPH3), 22q13.3.

Chromosome 2q37, 4q35.1-35.2, 8p23.2; chromosome 8p and 4q, P-glycoprotein gene (MDR1/ABCB1); glutamate transporter gene SLC1A1, IL1RAPL1 gene mutations, neuroligin mutants; SCAMP5, CLIC4 and PPCDC; fatty acid-binding protein (FABP7), 5-HT transporter gene (HTT, SERT, SLC6A4); proteins neurexin1 and PSD95; Cav3.2 T-type channels, chromosome 7q22-31 region; neuroligin-4 missense mutation; ADRA1A, ARHGEF10, CHRNA2, CHRNA6, CHRNB3, DKK4, DPYSL2, EGR3, FGF17, FGF20, FGFR1, FZD3, LDL, NAT2, NEF3, NRG1, PCM1, PLAT, PPP3CC, SFRP1, VMAT1; SLC18A1, microcephalin 1 gene (MCPH1).

Genetic polymorphisms of cytochrome P450 enzymes, 2p15-16.1, neurobeachin (Nbea); rs1858830 C allele variant, 3q26.31, serotonin receptor 2A gene (HTR2A); 1q42 deletion involving DISC1, DISC2, and TSNAX; alpha4beta 2 nicotinic acetylcholine receptors, adenosine A(2A) receptor gene (ADORA2A) variants; chromosome 1p34.2p34.3, synaptic vesicle gene RIMS3; microdeletions at 17q21.31, linkage loci on chromosomes 7 and 2; 2q37.3 deletion, neuroligin-3 R451C mutation; 2q24-2q31, 7q, 17q11-17q21; synaptic genes NLGN3, NLGN4, and

CNTNAP2; dysfunctional ERK and PI3K signaling, ribosomal protein L10 (RPL10) gene, glutamate decarboxylase gene 1 (GAD1) located within chromosome 2q31.

Breakpoints on chromosomes 5 and 18; short arm of chromosome 20, chromosome 20p12.2, serotonin receptor genes HTR1B and HTR2C; genes at 3q25-27, deletion of chromosome 2p25.2, chromosome 10, chromosome 1q21.1; Joubert syndrome gene (AHI1), deletion in 6q16.1, including GPR63 and FUT9; duplication of 8p23.1-8p23.2, NLGN4Y gene, inverted duplication of proximal chromosome 14; SYNGAP1, DLGAP2, X-linked DDX53-PTCHD1 locus; interstitial deletion 9q31.2 to q33.1, methyl-CpG binding protein 1; balanced de novo translocation between chromosomes 2 and 9; contactin 4 (CNTN4), chromosome 2q24-q33 region, PAX6 gene; deletion on 18q12, chromosome 5q31, PTEN, 13q21.

Microdeletions at 7q11.23, chromosomes 1p, 4p, 6q, 7q, 13q, 15q, 16p, 17q, 19q, 22q; FMR1 protein, FOXP2 gene; 2q35 and 8q21.2 breakpoint, sodium channels SCN1A, SCN2A and SCN3A; paternally derived chromosome 13, somatostatin receptor 5 (SSTR5) on chromosome 16p13.3; terminal 11q deletion and a distal 12q duplication, APOE protein, allelic variants of HOXA1/HOXB1; notch4 gene polymorphisms, AVP receptor 1a (AVPR1a), mitochondrial aspartate/ glutamate carrier SLC25A12 gene; Arg451Cys-neuroligin-3 mutation, language loci on chromosomes 2, 7, and 13; de novo translocation t(5;18)(q33.1;q12.1), p11.2p12.2.

Mu-opioid receptor gene, chromosome 16p13.3, trisomy 15q25.2-qter; 14q32.3 deletion, autism loci on 17q and 19p, linkage at 17q11-17q21, linkage on 21q and 7q; 3q29 microdeletion, haplotypes in the gene encoding protein kinase c-beta (PRKCB1) on chromosome 16; 6p25.3-22.3, SLC25A12 and CMYA3 gene variants; chromosome 3q25-27, inversion inv(4)(p12-p15.3), partial trisomy of chromosome 8p; locus in 15q14 region, terminal deletion of 4q, duplication at Xp11.22-p11.23; SEMA5A expression Tachykinin 1 (TAC1) gene SNPs, TPH2 and GLO1; biallelic PRODH mutation, recurrent 10q22-q23 deletions, neuropilin-2 (NRP2) gene polymorphisms.

Yes, I know—it might have taken less space to list the genetic features scientists have *not* implicated in autism's etiology.

Putrefaction

The modern scientist, with an air of superiority, will often extol the steady and methodical pace of scientific progress. But consider the work of Newton, Darwin, Einstein—what was steady and methodical about *that*?

The systematic advance of science is the smell of science gone bad.

Fresh Air

When nearly everyone has become lost in examining the details on all the barks of all the trees, the one who maps the forest performs a great and thankless task. Furthermore, the one who charts the territory *surrounding* the forest, he does an even greater and still *more* thankless task. And furthermore, the one who dares to whisper that there might be insight to be gained from the forest and its surrounding territory— and not from the barks of all the trees—he gets to play the role of today's pariah (and tomorrow's savior).

When the problem has become intractable, the way out is to examine the context. Digging deeper into the details only clouds the landscape with dust.

Scientific Insight

What level of research grant supported Newton's *Principia* project? What funding organization sponsored Darwin's laboratory of origined species? Who footed all the bills during Einstein's *Annus Mirabilis*?

Why is it that the forgettable science requires hundreds of thousands of dollars and entails an unspecified amount of time, whereas the memorable science costs barely a cent, and happens in little more than a flash?

The Uninspired Profession

When modern scientists begin talking process, design and methodology, I know that science has left the room.

Darwin's Corpse

I sometimes feel as though I have been sent here, ill-equipped as I am, to reclaim science from all the scientists. I awake each morning and sense that Darwin has been somehow kidnapped, tortured and murdered, and the duty has fallen upon me to go retrieve his mutilated corpse.

Take this passage from Steven Pinker's *The Language Instinct* (Pinker 1994), enough to make any admirer of Darwin utterly despair:

> "Evolution often produces spectacular abilities when adversaries get locked into an "arms race," like the struggle between cheetahs and gazelles. Some anthropologists believe that human brain evolution was propelled more by a cognitive arms race among social competitors than by mastery of technology and the physical environment. After all, it doesn't take that much brain power to master the ins and outs of a rock or to get the better of a berry. But outwitting and second-guessing an organism of approximately equal mental abilities with non-overlapping interests, at best, and malevolent intentions, at worst, makes formidable and ever-escalating demands on cognition."

Of the many problems plaguing evolutionary psychologists, certainly none can be more troubling than this collectively appalling grasp of evolution. It is as though all have found themselves the summertime denizens of a freshman remedial biology class, and have decided to make a *cause célèbre* out of their combined ignorance.

Why Life Is Not a Team Sport

The real conflict is not between science and religion, the real conflict is between collective ignorance and an individual sense of wonder. And in *that* conflict Dawkins, the Pope, Behe, Hitchens, Dobson, Harris, Dembski, Grayling, Dennett, and the grand ayatollahs are all on the same side.

Evolutionary Theory Versus Creationism

When I happen upon two third-graders engaged in a heated argument about whose dad is the best, I walk on past. I am an adult now.

Six Thousand Years Old

If we are speaking of the age of the world as humanity currently perceives it—with all our science, mathematics, literature, art, engineering, astronomy, and so on—then the creationists are certainly being far more accurate in their dating techniques than the evolutionists are. Six thousand years ago, this species had made considerable progress stepping in off the hunter-gatherer's grassy plain, but still lived much nearer to that plain than to our current forms of modern civilization. In Mesopotamia, Egypt, India, China—dazzling and remarkable transformations were on the verge of sudden bloom, transformations our scientists *still* have not characterized accurately, for those transformations have overwhelmed our scientists' means. To say that the world was created almost miraculously out of nothing beginning around six thousand years ago would not be pressing credibility any appreciable degree—not if we are regarding that world through the gaze of our own eyes.

If scientists can take any consolation from their miscalculation, it is that only *they* recognize such transformations must have a context in which to bloom—to deny the steadfast background of the soil is no better than to suppress wonderment at the germination of the seed. The mistake of the creationists has been to deny the very real context upon which this planet's miraculous transformation has taken place, and the mistake of the scientists has been to remain dogmatically blind to the fact that an anti-evolutionary transformation has happened at all.

Beasts

Evolution is a delicate description.
Bordering on the tautological,
It requires nuanced reflection
Upon time, environment and biological dynamics
To see its process unfolding as physical necessity,
And not deductive creed.

Thus when lumbering, blustery giants
Such as Dawkins and Pinker barge in,
One is reminded of stubbly-thumbed oafs
Who destroy posthaste every delicacy they touch.
No subtlety. No discretion. Just
The ponderous pounding of their shiny new toy
Again and again and again.

It is that trait,
This barbarous, incontinent bashing
Of Darwin's dangerous idea
Against every surface they meet,
That betrays their vulnerability—
Like beasts,
They have not reflected upon evolution at all.

Naïve

In 1905, a young patent office clerk submitted for publication a straightforward essay—*On the Electrodynamics of Moving Bodies*. Apparently oblivious as to how these things are done, he failed to enlist the services of recognized co-authors, and forgot to include a pile of citations from the leading scientific personalities of his time. I can only assume it was the most egregious of editorial board snafus that allowed that clerk's essay to see the light of day.

The Problem with Peer Review

Genuine scientists, the ones who unveil surprising, valuable and enduring insights into our experienced world—scientists such as Newton, Darwin and Einstein—they of course have no peers. Career scientists on the other hand, the ones who travel at the speed of the imitative infinitesimal, they are to be found around every street corner, and of course filling out all the editorial review boards.

Authorship Litany

Here is the list of co-authors from a paper recently published in a prestigious autism research journal: A. Mulligan, R. J. L. Anney, M. O'Regan, W. Chen, L. Butler, M. Fitzgerald, J. Buitelaar, H. Steinhausen, A. Rothenberger, R. Minderaa, J. Nijmeijer, P. J. Hoekstra, R. D. Oades, H. Roeyers, C. Buschgens, H. Christiansen, B. Franke, I. Gabriels, C. Hartman, J. Kuntsi, R. Marco, S. Meidad, U. Mueller, L. Psychogiou, N. Rommelse, M. Thompson, H. Uebel, T. Banaschewski, R. Ebstein, J. Eisenberg, I. Manor, A. Miranda, F. Mulas, J. Sergeant, E. Sonuga-Barke, P. Asherson, S. V. Faraone, M. Gill.

Now you might be thinking I have exaggerated that list, or at the very least have cherry picked the most egregious example of piled-on authorship I could find. But rest assured, the above example is actually quite tame—there are many other instances just like it, and some much worse. The journal *Nature*, for instance, has made a regular habit in recent years of publishing autism research papers sporting authorship lists running into the several score—even into the hundreds. And this does not count the considerable acknowledgements sections, raising the question of how much contribution actually *merits* an acknowledgement for such a paper, seeing as how it could not garner a spot on the enormous front page list.

As an outsider, I find myself perplexed by one particular aspect of this practice. In the reckoning of official publishing credit—the kind that can be cashed in for tenure, grants, editorial board appointments, offices with a nice view, and so forth (what would appear to be the most challenging goals in the field of autism research)—does an author get one full credit for having his or her name attached to such a copious list, or does the publishing credit get divided evenly throughout all the list's members? Because if the latter, I am having a hard time understanding how 1/38th of a publishing credit can go very far. Speaking strictly for myself, if I found I had to participate in thirty-eight such enterprises to earn one full credit, I might find it easier just to do some original work and write it up on my own.

Covering the Costs of Autism Research Publication

I would like to propose a new approach to paying for the costs of autism research publication: instead of having subscribers pay for *access* to autism research journals, a much better solution would be to have contributors pay for the right to *publish* in autism research journals.

This idea might appear at first glance to be somewhat counterintuitive, but it has one obvious advantage over the current approach—the new approach does a much better job of matching costs to benefits. For example, *readers* of autism research journals, who currently receive nothing of value for their enterprise, would no longer be charged for that dubious privilege, providing in this case a perfect match of expense and gain. At the same time, those who get *published* in autism research journals—and thereby gain access to tenured positions, editorial board appointments, government committees, and of course additional funding—they would be obliged to provide a reasonable amount of recompense for these many benefits, thereby helping to keep the system going.

But I believe I can do this excellent idea even one better.

Instead of charging a flat fee for the publication of an autism research article, a more effective approach would be to charge an exponentially increasing scale based upon the number of co-authors listed on each paper. A one-author article, for instance—which after all does have *some* chance of providing valuable insights into the nature of autism—might be published for just a nominal amount, or perhaps even for free. Adding a second author, however, would require the expenditure of, say, an additional two thousand dollars at the final invoice; adding a third author would augment the overall fee by a further four thousand dollars; adding a fourth author would cost an additional eight thousand dollars, and so on.

Under this proposal—and given the size of some authorship lists I have seen on *recent* autism articles—a few lucky journals might find themselves able to cover an entire decade's worth of expense with the publication of a single article alone. However, let me be clear on this, I do not recommend the booking of outlandish profits under such circumstances: revenue gathered in excess of reasonable costs should be returned to the supporting governmental agencies, for the express purpose of retiring national debts.

Another feature that might be added to my proposal—a slight enhancement, if you will—would be to require a surcharge for the inclusion of co-authors who possess high name recognition or who have reached a certain standard of publication profligacy. That is to say, for each S. Baron-Cohen, G. Dawson, or F. Volkmar pasted onto the end of any given co-authorship list, this would add, say, an additional fifty thousand dollars to the final publishing fee. Now it is true that if this supplemental S. Baron-Cohen, G. Dawson, or F. Volkmar happens to be the tenth author "contributing" to the given paper, then that additional name, under the scale described above, would already be setting the paper back to the tune of a half million dollars or so, and thus tacking on an *additional* fifty thousand dollars might seem like overdoing it a bit. But keep in mind that the value in this new approach is to match costs to benefits, and we all know how much a career (not to mention, the peer review prospects) can be enhanced by association with that one special "colleague." If perhaps this final feature of my proposal seems a bit too controversial, might I suggest employing it on a trial basis at first (for instance, with G. Dawson alone), until its asset enhancing benefits become more apparent.

I of course have some additional revenue raising suggestions, ones based upon the number of citations employed in each article—in particular, citations of the authors' own previous work—but I would prefer to keep such suggestions on the back burner for now; I do not want to overload the system all at once with too much cash. After appropriate investment plans have been put in place at each journal, along with the safeguards against pilferage, then maybe consideration can be given to some of these more advanced techniques.

Now I know what you must be thinking. You must be thinking that if this new approach is so obviously beneficial, then why has someone from the autism research community not suggested it before. I admit to feeling a bit sheepish about having to make this proposal myself, being an outsider and all, but I would note that there are many circumstances in which those who are part of a community are so attached to that community they cannot easily take a step back and gain some proper perspective. Quite often—let us be honest here for once—people are standing too close to the problem to recognize its solution.

Futuristic Vision

I can see where this co-authorship thing is heading. One day, in the not too distant future, a paper will appear entitled *Today*, consisting of a single sentence: "We did some stuff." The authorship list will comprise the names of the six billion some human inhabitants on this planet, and the paper will be published in the journal *Nature*, which seems to have a hankering for these things. Everyone can then go about their business of applying for tenure, comfortable in the knowledge it cannot be denied.

I hope that day comes soon; in fact, it cannot arrive fast enough. Because then maybe someone—anyone—will finally feel free enough to develop an idea on his own.

When Science Goes a Whoring

It is not for idle purpose that I shine a light on the community of autism research journals. The attitudes backing practices of piled-on authorship, sycophantic peer review, citation back-scratching and editorial board nepotism are the very antithesis of science. (And I have yet to mention the harm being done to autistic individuals.)

Identification Bias

Because autism was first taken to be a medical condition—a type of serious mental illness—its ongoing recognition has always suffered from a very bad case of identification bias.

Around forty to fifty years ago, the only cases of autism being diagnosed were those for which the individual was clearly detached from usual behaviors and circumstances, and was clearly in need of support and services. This practice made sense then, because at that time autism was assumed to be an acute medical condition and therefore only individuals meeting the *criteria* of an acute medical condition could be identified as having autism. No one else was identified as having autism, and of course autism was thought to be extremely rare.

However, a problem soon emerged. The medical community began recognizing many individuals who possessed most of the same features as those being diagnosed with autism, but who obviously were not suffering from an acute medical condition. This should have alerted the medical community that its initial assumption about autism *being* a medical condition was now seriously in doubt; but identification bias had already set in, had become too firmly entrenched, and no serious questioning of that assumption ever took place. When one reads for instance the work of Lorna Wing, which started the process of bringing Asperger syndrome into the diagnostic fold, one is struck immediately by how the new criteria, although distinguished from the criteria used on the more classically diagnosed cases, still assumed a major underlying cognitive impairment, still assumed the presence of a serious medical condition. And so, as terms such as *high-functioning autism, Asperger syndrome*, and *pervasive developmental disorder* began to assume more widespread usage, the specter of medical illness never loosened its grip on autism at all—that specter merely began enveloping a much larger population within its darkening fold.

That trend continues unabated to the present day. Using an expanding range of diagnostic tools and applying them at earlier and earlier ages, the medical community now identifies nearly one percent of the toddler population as possessing some form of autism, and because of identification bias, that entire one percent is assumed to be suffering from a dire medical condition. With no consideration for whether the expected outcome might be positive or negative, and with no recall of the statistics from its own diagnosing past, the medical community assumes each child identified as being autistic will require a regimen of early intervention and will need an onslaught of powerful drugs, intensive therapies, and assorted preventative treatments. It never occurs to the medical community that its own history of autism identification has now passed from rare to questionable to absurd. It never dawns on the medical community that nearly the entire one percent now being identified as mentally ill, was only one half century ago being identified with nary a sickness at all.

It is not too late to turn back the clock, even some fifty years. Autism has *never* been a medical condition: that stranglehold of an assumption is only the residue from a lazy history of bias.

The Many Autisms

A growing trend within the autism research community is to characterize autism not as a single condition but instead as a constellation of many different conditions, each with a distinct etiology (albeit an *unknown* etiology). But the actual source of this so-called theory of the many autisms is not scientific insight. The actual source of this theory is embarrassment.

These days the autism research community produces a near constant flood of announcements—a new set almost every day—each loudly proclaiming the latest breakthrough in such areas as genetics, pharmacology, neuroimaging and treatments. An *occasional* such announcement would of course be greeted with enthusiasm and interest, but the steady *flood* of such announcements, many of them mutually exclusive, soon begins to sound downright humiliating. How significant can any of these breakthroughs be when each is just one more being added to a swelling crowd.

Unwilling to admit that this flood of breakthrough announcements is the most compelling evidence yet for their *lack* of understanding, autism scientists conceal their embarrassment by trotting out the theory of the many autisms. Each announcement remains significant, they insist, because each announcement introduces yet another unique and newly minted *type* of autism, one more autism in the pantheon of the many autisms. *Voilà!*

And so rather than gathering knowledge *about* autism, scientists instead pile up the many autisms and hope no one will notice the difference. But like the child who gets caught in a lie, and attempts to avoid the consequences by weaving still more lies, these researchers who resort to the theory of the many autisms will one day discover they have merely compounded their embarrassment.

A Foretold History of Autism Science

It is hard to scale a phantom mountain. Inevitably, that climbing party must come back down.

Scientific Accumulation

A million trivial results do not add up to something significant; they add up to triviality.

Lost and Found

Professor Simon Baron-Cohen and his colleagues have written concernedly about today's "lost generation" of adults who are just now being diagnosed—long after their childhood has ended—with various forms of autism (usually Asperger Syndrome):

> "But what of the generation who were born before 1980, who may have had Asperger Syndrome but for whom there was no diagnosis available? No specialist clinical teams, not even the concept of Asperger Syndrome. How did they fare? The answer is that they were overlooked, and struggled through their school years. And the reason we run a clinic for the very late diagnosis of Asperger Syndrome is because these are the lost generation: those who today would receive their diagnosis by 6 or 8 years old, if they were a 21st century child. They come to our clinic in young adulthood or even middle age, and they tell us a now-familiar story.
>
> "All through their school years they had trouble making friends or fitting in. Many were bullied by the other children, both physically and verbally. Many felt, in Claire Sainsbury's chilling words, like "an alien in the playground". (This is the title of her excellent book). The lucky ones managed to stay in school long enough to get their SATs, and some got to university. But not without feeling their teens were an uphill struggle. By young adulthood many had suffered clinical depression and even felt suicidal. All because their underlying condition of Asperger Syndrome had gone unrecognized and therefore unsupported. Some of them had enjoyed the closeness of an intimate relationship only for this to break down. Some had found employment only for them to run into problems in the work place through not understanding what the employer and other staff might expect of them, or through getting into conflict, or being passed over for promotion because of their lack of team skills." (Baron-Cohen et al. 2007)

But there must be something grossly amiss in Baron-Cohen's description. The above paragraphs imply that there has been only *one* lost generation of autistic adults, the generation born right before 1980. But how can that possibly be? What about the previous generation, those who were born in the 1950s and 1960s? Or what about those who were born in the early 1900s? Or those who were born in the 1800s, and even much earlier than that? Does Baron-Cohen mean to suggest that autism descended *en masse* upon humanity sometime in the late twentieth century, and are we meant to understand there were no autistic adults living among us until a few began showing up outside the door of his clinic—desperate for relief (or so he says) from the wretched circumstances he and his colleagues would have thrust upon them?

This generation of autistic adults Baron-Cohen is attempting to describe can only be the latest in an impressively long line of autistic generations, a line reaching far back into humanity's ancient past. And that autism has gone unrecognized for so long in fact suggests exactly the opposite of what Baron-Cohen is so concernedly trying to say—it suggests that there has been nothing lost, or even wretched, about any of these prior generations. Far from being *lost*, the current generation of autistic adults is indeed the first to be *found*—found living quietly and productively among us, as autistic generations always have. But if Baron-Cohen and his colleagues must insist on hunting for those who have supposedly gone astray, might I suggest they expand their search beyond their clinic door. For out in nearly every street can be found a generation of autistic adults much larger than even Baron-Cohen has managed to conceive, a generation doing well enough it would never think to bother with his self-deluded clinic.

As I have written elsewhere, autism has had a significant presence within the human population for a very long time—a presence mostly silent, yet not without consequence.

Control Group

In clinical trials of autism treatment options, why has no researcher ever thought to make use of the most obvious control group—those autistic individuals who have escaped diagnosis? Really, it should be a simple matter to round them up from the various institutions, graveyards and other dumping grounds of irretrievably broken lives.

Or has it been not that easy to track them down?

Thanks—Now Here's the Back of Our Hand

It remains amazing to me how articulate autistic children can be, and remains equally amazing to me how dense and cruel autism scientists can be in response.

In the spring of 2009, press releases were widely circulated regarding the results of a report published in the journal *Nature*, *Two-year-olds with Autism Orient to Non-social Contingencies Rather than Biological Motion* (Klin et al. 2009). The report's introduction reads as follows:

> "Typically developing human infants preferentially attend to biological motion within the first days of life. This ability is highly conserved across species and is believed to be critical for filial attachment and for detection of predators. The neural underpinnings of biological motion perception are overlapping with brain regions involved in perception of basic social signals such as facial expression and gaze direction, and preferential attention to biological motion is seen as a precursor to the capacity for attributing intentions to others. However, in a serendipitous observation, we recently found that an infant with autism failed to recognize point-light displays of biological motion, but was instead highly sensitive to the presence of a non-social, physical contingency that occurred within the stimuli by chance. This observation raised the possibility that perception of biological motion may be altered in children with autism from a very early age, with cascading consequences for both social development and the lifelong impairments in social interaction that are a hallmark of autism spectrum disorders. Here we show that two-year-olds with autism fail to orient towards point-light displays of biological motion, and their viewing behaviour when watching these point-light displays can be explained instead as a response to non-social, physical contingencies— physical contingencies that are disregarded by control children. This observation has far-reaching implications for understanding the altered neurodevelopmental trajectory of

brain specialization in autism. This study points in a number of interesting directions."

The report goes on to describe the study in more detail, outlining how autistic children and control groups were shown side-by-side videos of point-light animations formed from scenarios played out by human actors, with one display being shown right side up and forwards running in time (so that the light points had some resemblance to human motion), the other display being shown upside down and running backwards in time (so that the light points had random appearance and were not synchronized to the accompanying sound track). Using eye gaze for measure, the researchers first demonstrated that non-autistic controls showed more preference for the right-side-up display, whereas autistic children seemed to show no particular preference for either display. This apparently was the original purpose of the study, to demonstrate that non-autistic children have a "normal," and therefore "healthy," response to biological motion, whereas autistic children do not have a similar response—just one more wood chip on the autism-as-disorder lumber pile.

However, in one of the trials, in which the human actor was playing pat-a-cake (with the clapping sound prominent on the sound track), the researchers noticed that a fifteen-month-old autistic girl—who in the other trials showed no particular preference for either display—revealed in this instance a clear and intense preference for the upright image. Since it was only in the upright image that the clapping sound corresponded to the motions of the point-light display, the researchers wondered if it was the synchronized clapping that the autistic girl was responding to, and after re-examining all their data and after developing further trials to confirm this "serendipitous" discovery, the researchers concluded that a preference for non-biological pattern was consistent and significant across the entire autistic group.

Notice what has happened. Due to the articulate response of one autistic child (along with the corroborating responses of her autistic cohorts), the overall findings of this study were greatly improved from what they otherwise would have been. The findings could now be summarized in the following manner:

- Non-autistic toddlers respond preferably to human biological motion, and do not respond preferably to non-biological pattern.
- Autistic toddlers respond preferably to non-biological pattern, and do not respond preferably to human biological motion.
- Neither group responds preferably to random sensory noise.

Although these findings are not nearly as new as the report's press releases would have us believe (they are consistent with many other findings regarding the primary distinction between autistic and non-autistic perception), the study's enhanced conclusions are at least more valuable than they would have been based on what the researchers initially had in mind, for the enhanced conclusions provide a more accurate picture of what autistic perception actually *is*, as opposed to just another worn-out description of what autistic perception is *not* (not to mention, the enhanced results add also to our knowledge of non-autistic perception). It would seem therefore that the study's researchers owe an extreme debt of gratitude to that one articulate autistic girl, the one who pointed them in the right direction, the one who helped them see what had actually been in front of their eyes all along.

So how did the members of the autism research community decide to repay this debt of gratitude? Why, they repaid this child in the same way autism researchers have *always* responded to articulate autistic children—they gave her the back of their hand.

Here is a sampling of quotations given in response to the Klin et al. study:

From Ami Klin, the study's lead author: "Our hope is to detect vulnerabilities for autism as early as possible, so as to intervene with the hope to capitalize on the babies' brain malleability."

From Thomas Insel, Director of the National Institute of Mental Health: "For the first time, this study has pinpointed what grabs the attention of toddlers with [autism spectrum disorders]. In addition to potential uses in screening for early diagnosis, this line of research holds promise for development of new therapies based on redirecting visual attention in children with these disorders."

From Geraldine Dawson, Chief Science Officer of Autism Speaks, an autism charity group devoted to the distinctly uncharitable task of curing and/or eradicating autism: "These findings could potentially be useful in detecting infants at risk for autism very early in life. It is important to use therapeutic strategies for children with autism that help draw their attention to people, including their facial expressions, and gestures."

Let me see if I have this straight. This young autistic girl, along with her study group cohorts, has helped open these researchers' eyes to the fact that autistic individuals do not have randomly damaged perception, but instead respond positively, consistently and *usefully* to a particular form of stimulus that can be found regularly within their environment, but the researchers' one and only response to this discovery is to suggest forcible removal of this preferred form of perception from autistic children and to offer instead mass substitution of the one type of stimulus autistic children have markedly demonstrated they do *not* respond to. Absolutely amazing.

Note that if I were to suggest that *non-autistic* children could be greatly improved by forcibly redirecting them away from biological and social stimuli and towards a non-stop bombardment of pattern-based perceptions, this while their brains were still malleable enough to be re-formed, I would be decried for both my *folly* and my *cruelty*. But somehow, when that same corresponding approach is suggested for autistic children, it is considered to be the height of modern scientific insight, is considered to be the epitome of good autism science.

Sadly enough, so it is.

My hope is that one day, after that articulate autistic girl has had the opportunity to grow up and comes to understand what kind of blind, aping response was made to her, she is able to track down those so-called scientists Klin, Insel and Dawson, and in the literal manner autistic individuals are apt to prefer, she gives them the back of *her* hand.

The intellectual and moral bankruptcy of autism science has never been more apparent.

Tsunami

As harmful as bad science has been to autistic individuals (and that harm has been considerable) it is a mere drop in the bucket compared to the damage inflicted under the heading of good science. Good science has been the tsunami washing across every autistic land, leaving behind an ever expanding legacy of destruction and mayhem.

What autistic peace was disturbed when good science crashed ashore?

The Takeaway from Autism Science

If you cannot conceive the context, and if you have no grasp of the concept, then all the material data in the world will serve only to feed your blindness. Even *good* information turns rancid in the oppressive heat of ignorance.

Humanity

Autism as Offense

I.

"The moment when an individual is unwilling to subordinate himself to the established order or indeed even questions its being true, yes, charges it with being untruth, whereas he declares that he himself is in the truth and of the truth, declares that the truth lies specifically in inwardness—then there is the collision." (Kierkegaard, *Practice in Christianity*)

The autism industry is both popular and large. From autism scientists (all too happy to promote their latest breakthrough, treatment or cure) to autism charity groups (all too happy to raise the next dollar for their "non-profit" coffers) to government officials (all too happy to sponsor namesake legislation credited with easing autism's burden)—every direction one turns, one can find yet another crowd jumping onto the autism-as-blight bandwagon. And who would dare blame them? Because if anything stands as an affront to normalcy, it would have to be autism—that paragon of abnormality. If anything stands as an outrage against the status quo, it would have to be autism—that epitome of deviation. If anything stands as an insult to the bandwagon-jumping crowd, it would have to be autism—that apex of going it alone. Thus we hear the mantra being repeated incessantly throughout the land: autism is a disease, autism is a disorder, autism is a tragedy, autism must be stopped. Many reputations and livelihoods now depend upon that mantra and upon its incessant repetition.

But should an autistic individual defy this established order, confront this multitude, set himself apart as one against the many, shout loudly enough to be heard against authority's command, "No, you are all wrong, completely wrong. I am not diseased, not disordered, not a tragedy, I will not be stopped. Autism's truth is to be discovered by listening to those like me, because autism's truth is *within* me, *from* me, *of* me. Let me *show* you what this condition can be, let me *demonstrate* what autism can do." Should this individual be so defiant as to draw attention to himself, he will be met by the bandwagon-jumping crowd with derision, with intervention, with demands he be treated and cured. He will damn near be crucified.

Autism is a rebellious god, and thus continues to offend.

II.

"He wants to save all, but in order to be saved they must go through the possibility of offense—ah, it is as if he, the savior who wants to save all, came to stand almost alone because everyone is offended at him."

Not that long ago humanity lived as little more than animal, a cognitive and behavioral slave to survival and procreation alone, and left to the *typical* forms of species-driven perception, man would still be living as little more than animal to this day. But come hither, my friend. Come hither and hear the good news, for autism has brought forth a miraculous transformation. With their perceptions not dominated by species-specific focus, with their perceptions now liberated to recognize the pattern, structure and form of the surrounding, non-biological world, autistic individuals have brought forth the power of atypicality, have brought forth the splendor of paradigm-shifting vision, have brought forth the majesty of rebellious upheaval, have brought forth the miracle of continuous human surprise. In a mere sliver of time—a sliver of time so short it must have left evolutionary history gasping with awe—man has ridden the strength of these strange new perceptions straight in off the hunter-gatherer's grassy plain, straight forwards in search of an entire universe.

But should an autistic individual make proud note of these achievements, appeal to these autistic merits, herald these autistic strengths, announce pressingly the good news to a disbelieving, rejecting public, "But don't you see, it has always been the *atypical* vision that has advanced human understanding, forwarded the human condition. Just look at all the great innovators—Archimedes, Michelangelo, Newton, Beethoven, Turing—not a typical individual among them, only those who have lived far outside the human norm. Do not look to your commonest neighbor, look instead to the unusual one standing apart—

there you will find the key to humanity's unprecedented turn." Should this individual be so pressing as to draw attention to himself, he will be met by the disbelieving, rejecting public with strong words of their own: "Foolish lout! Deluded bastard! Arrogant lunatic!" They will practically spit the words right into his face.

Autism is an accomplished god, and thus continues to offend.

III.

"That a human being falls into the power of his enemies and does nothing, that is human. But that the one whose almighty hand had done signs and wonders, that he now stands there powerless and paralyzed—precisely this is what brings him to be denied."

Autism presents grave challenges. Because autistic individuals do not readily perceive and attach to other humans, because they cannot easily organize their experiences around the species itself and around what other people do, autistic individuals find themselves detached from the human population, right from a very early age. Deprived of the *typical* means of development, autistic individuals of necessity mature slowly and awkwardly. Deprived of the *typical* means of sensory organization, autistic individuals must struggle through an assortment of sensory difficulties. The non-autistic population—so easily in tune with one another, so naturally aware of what other people do, so effortlessly imitative of nearly everyone around them—judges autistic detachment to be a sign of sickness, evidence of a tragic defect. Stubbornly unconvinced that autistic individuals can organize their perceptions in an entirely different manner (a manner which has created profound benefit for the entire human population), the non-autistic population demands of autistic individuals that they learn to perceive and behave exactly as everyone else, and when this effort ultimately fails (as fail it must), autistic individuals are written off as broken, written off as a burden, written off as completely without hope.

But should an autistic individual request a modicum of understanding, ask that his progress be measured by his own standard, seek permission to mature at his own pace, beseech desperately for an ounce of approval from the disapproving throng, "But please, be charitable—my atypicality is not just my strength, it is my weakness as well. Allow me more time, offer me some patience, give me the opportunity to raise myself by my own unusual means." Should this individual be so beseeching as to draw attention to himself, he will be met by the disapproving throng with a shake of its collective head, with the back of its collective hand: "Your unusual means are the evidence of your sickness, they are what prevents you from being competent just like us. If not so, then prove yourself, heal yourself, support yourself— make your so-called grandeur evident at this very moment, make your powerful abilities apparent so that all can plainly see." In the silence that immediately follows, both the disappointment and the mockery are ready made.

Autism is a humbled god, and thus continues to offend.

Invoice

In *The Costs of Autism* (Ganz 2006), Professor Michael Ganz estimates the burden of autism on the United States economy to be around thirty-five billion dollars per year.

But of course with both a presumed autism epidemic and inflation running amok, surely it would not be asking too much to at least double that amount, to keep the number more currently up to date. And furthermore, the United States is just one country—a populous and expensive country, true, but one country nonetheless—and thus it would not be stretching the seams of Ganz's figure too greatly to apply an additional factor of ten when calculating a more worldwide estimate. And finally for rounding sake, if nothing else, we might as well nudge the total to a full one trillion dollars per year; because when it comes to this side of the balance sheet, I think it is only prudent we not appear too stingy.

Then let us consider a simple list of individuals—a partial list, true, but on *this* side of the balance sheet there is no need to be too greedy. Newton, Socrates, Darwin, Michelangelo, Luther, Archimedes, Van Gogh, Dostoyevsky, Kierkegaard, Beethoven, Einstein, Turing. I believe it has been well documented the amount of recompense these individuals have received for their various efforts, an amount generally understood to be somewhat short of modest.

Thus if Ganz is going to insist on a settling of accounts, and the agreement is that the worldwide autistic burden runs to a full one trillion dollars per year, then I think an obvious question still remains: when does the autistic population receive the remainder of what is due?

Diagnosis Is the Wrong Word

We commonly say that autism is diagnosed, but the word *diagnosis* rests on a shaky foundation, the danger of which is never more evident than when we promote early diagnoses for young children.

To use the word *diagnosis* is to accept the assumption that autism is a medical condition or a mental illness; but this is precisely the assumption most in doubt. The medical community, which on one hand acts with unbridled certainty that autism is indeed a mental disorder and a brain-based illness, on the other hand admits that the cause of autism remains entirely unknown with no known effective cure. So where does that certainty come from in the first place?

What if autism were not a medical condition, not a mental illness? Would we still be able to discern that possibility, given that we have already put the blinders on?

Those who speak favorably of early diagnosis inevitably follow with the phrase *early intervention*. But how can early intervention be considered safe and effective if there is no known cause of autism? How can early intervention be deemed appropriate if we remain uncertain of what autism is? The treatment of a non-existent illness is not necessarily benign.

Not all that long ago the diagnosis of autism was an extremely rare event. Are we certain that those who went undiagnosed—and who therefore went untreated—are we certain their outcomes were inevitably tragic?

The correct word is *recognition*. These days, we know enough about autism to *recognize* it in certain individuals, including some who are very young. But recognition is all we have.

The Difficulty in Recognizing Autism for What It Is

There exists a class of people—by current estimates totaling approximately one percent of the human population—whose members possess a condition fundamentally distinguishing the class from the remainder of the species.

- Some of the class's members are diagnosed with the condition in early childhood, usually at five years of age or less; these members are commonly labeled *autistic.*
- Some of the class's members are diagnosed in late childhood or during adolescence, roughly between the ages of six and eighteen; these members are frequently labeled *Asperger's.*
- Some of the class's members are diagnosed only after reaching adulthood; these are often described as being *schizophrenic* or *bipolar.*

Notice the word "diagnosis" in each of these descriptions—labeling occurs nearly always under conditions perceived to be psychiatricly negative. And note how the labels are a function of the *age* at diagnosis, and thus do not differentiate the underlying condition itself. Finally, note that the variable age of diagnosis suggests these labels do not complete the class: it is likely there are other members, perhaps a significantly large number, ones who do not get diagnosed or labeled at all.

The Certainty March

Of course left-handedness must be cured—it is the mark of the Devil!

Of course homosexuality must be cured—it is an abomination to God!

Of course autism must be cured—it is a kidnapping of the soul!

The Two-Thirds Rule

I am hesitant to put forth the two-thirds rule, because it is indeed the roughest of rules of thumb. But having found it helpful so far in my own parenting experience, and believing it might be of some service to others, I offer it here along with Thoreau's gentle admonition—that none stretch the seams in putting the garment on.

The two-thirds rule says that in development and maturation, particularly in those areas relating to acquisition of social and biological skills, autistic individuals will on average proceed at roughly two-thirds the pace of their non-autistic peers. Some autistics will be speedier, of course, while others will march to an even more measured beat. But as expectation, as seat-of-the-pants measuring, a two-thirds pace would appear to be a reasonable guide.

Examples of the rule's application might include:

- Toilet training: accomplished around three years of age by most, but more often hurdled near the age of five or six by many autistic individuals.
- Basic social language (spoken, gestured or typed): this shoots forth like a meteoric star in most children between the ages of two and five, but is acquired more deliberately by autistic children much closer to the ages of four to eight.
- Sexuality (with all its unwritten rules): of sudden and critical importance to many non-autistic individuals in their early teens; but more safely, effectively and willingly explored by autistic individuals much nearer to their late teens.
- The final rites of passage into adulthood (graduation, job, marriage, children): often approached impatiently as early as the age of sixteen by many, and yet for autistic individuals, it seems most are not yet ready for such endeavors, even by the age of twenty-one (which might explain why so many can be found hiding out in graduate school, or in their parents' spare room). When we speak of full adult maturation in the autistic population, we are probably speaking mid to late twenties, maybe even later.

The above examples notwithstanding, the two-thirds rule is not intended as a tool for comparison. It is intended primarily as a means for enhancing understanding, and as an encouragement towards a more liberal use of patience and time. There is no shame to be associated with proceeding at a two-thirds rate, or at any rate indeed. Maturation is not a race. The quality of the finished product is far more important than the speed at which any development occurs. Plus we should not forget that autistic individuals receive significant compensation for their tardiness in the social and biological realms. Outside these domains, and particularly in areas of special interests, autistics will often quickly surpass their non-autistic peers (and in some cases, will manage to transcend). And one further thing I have noticed: upon reaching adulthood—at whatever calendar age that may be—autistic individuals often feel no urge to pause. Having battled their maturity battle for so long, perhaps they find it only natural to keep right on going, whereas with many non-autistic individuals I know, they seem particularly vulnerable to getting stuck near the developmental age of seventeen, the remainder of their biological time played out as little more than a reminiscence of glory days.

For autistic individuals, their glory days always seem to be the ones still ahead.

One More Session

At first, he might even cooperate—
Longing for praise and uncertain yet
As to the nature of this new game,
He leaps forward with beaming curiosity.
You begin touting his sudden progress.

Later, after he has recognized
This falsely structured hour
As yet one more attempt
To pound a square peg into a round hole,
You begin searching for a new therapy.

Autism and Disability

The statement that autism is a disability can stir controversy, all the more so because the grammar of the word *disability* is itself imprecise. That imprecision notwithstanding, let me offer two observations I believe can shed some light on the subject:

- There are many autistic individuals who are not, have not been, and will not ever be disabled.
- There are many autistic individuals who are currently, have been in the past, and/or will be in the future disabled.

Those two assertions suggest that discussing the concept of autism alongside the concept of disability makes sense, but that *predicating* the concept of autism with the concept of disability is far less precise—if not downright erroneous. We do not entirely understand what produces disability in certain autistic individuals. Attributing that outcome to autism itself is only an assumption, and in my view, not a very good one.

The Telltale Origin of Time and Space

Recognition of non-biological symmetry, structure and pattern is the basis of the notions of time and space, and this recognition has not come easily, it is not natural to a species. Its first appearance on this planet occurred only a handful of millennia ago, and there are no indications of such recognition in the cognition and behaviors of the other animal species, or in the cognition and behaviors of early humans.

Thus the word *normalcy* does not attach to temporal and spatial recognition. To witness a spontaneous, biological occurrence of such recognition, one would need to look more carefully at the cognition and behaviors of those children we have ironically labeled as *disordered*.

Bicycle Built for Three

Autism, schizophrenia and bipolar disorder (manic depression) are listed separately in the *Diagnostic and Statistical Manual of Mental Disorders*, but a discerning eye will recognize the commonality among all these conditions:

- Each is classified as a mental illness without any evidence of sickness.
- Each is diagnosed through behavioral characteristics instead of direct etiology.
- Each manifests a cognitive perceptual focus distinct from the species-driven norm.

These three conditions are eerily similar, and to a misunderstanding humanity, they ride past as triplets in crime.

Ockham's Razor

This:

Autistic disorder, Asperger syndrome, childhood schizophrenia, pervasive developmental disorder, classic autism, high-functioning autism, low-functioning autism, bipolar disorder, non-verbal learning disability, savant syndrome, regressive autism, passing for normal, mistakenly diagnosed.

Or this:

One cognitive phenomenon—with outcomes ranging from tragic to sublime.

The Risk of Chelation and Lupron Therapy

When I hear testimonials from the proponents of chelation and lupron therapy, I am always surprised no mention is ever made of the potential risk involved. No, I do not mean the risk to the child's health or future well-being—I realize that risk can be dismissed easily enough, as it does not hit nearly close enough to home. But the inevitability of the coming lawsuit, how is that risk so blithely ignored?

The cases against the medical practitioners will be plausible *prima facie* and worth every possible attempt. And although the law would be much murkier here, an endeavor against the parents will almost certainly be given a go. Or to put it another way, in case I am failing to awaken those who desperately need to hear: if I were a young, aspiring and slightly hungry lawyer, and were hearing the details about the damage being done, I would be taking down names, birth dates and numbers, and warming up the phone.

These children are going to turn 21 one day, and upon that germination, the flower of litigation is surely going to bloom.

The Bracing Mountain Air

What a manic episode *Zarathustra* was. Just think, with some lithium or valproate, Nietzsche could have stayed calm for that week and a half.

Health Coverage

Many efforts are currently underway to mandate insurance and state coverage for various types of autism medical treatment. These efforts are premature.

Not in any way certain of the condition it is dealing with and ignoring its charge to first do no harm, the medical community has been offering up a dangerous and scattershot approach to autism treatment—oppressive applied behavioral analysis, overpowering pharmacology, random interventive therapies, plus a few doses of biomedical quackery thrown in for good measure. What these treatments have in common is that none are designed to promote autistic capacity—all are designed to shut it down.

When attitudes have changed, when humanity has understood autism for what it truly is, when medical efforts have turned away from suppression and cure and turned towards autistic achievement, only then will autism coverage become a worthwhile investment—not the drain of resources and human dignity that it currently is.

Kierkegaard as Educator

For that clique of oh-so cutting edge atheists (Dawkins, Hitchens, Harris, Dennett, and the remainder of their huddling masses)—I would have it take note of Kierkegaard, who standing all by himself did not choose the cowardly path of abolishing religious thought, but instead took fearless aim at what religion had become.

I too—I have not the slightest desire to put an end to scientific thought or practice, but merely draw a bead on what science has become.

Dawkins, Hitchens, Harris and Dennett

Short-sighted science, intellectual fatuousness, a simpleton's atheism—who needs to believe in a Hell's afterlife when we have the torturers themselves right here?

The Distinguished Professor of Philosophy

I could spend the remainder of my days railing against that absurdity known as modern academic philosophy, but let me save us the time and concentrate instead on one of its more fatuous examples—Professor A. C. Grayling.

I first stumbled upon Professor Grayling while he was still hacking out a career at the expense of an honest man:

> "Once one has sifted his texts and has ceased to be dazzled by the brilliance of metaphor and the poetical quality, one finds much less argument, and very much less definiteness in the crucial conceptions, than is expected in and demanded from philosophical enquiry. This is disappointing." (Grayling 1988)

I hold little hope for the present age, but I trust history will forever enjoy the irony of that self-assured lecture—Professor A. C. Grayling passing his eternal judgment upon Ludwig Wittgenstein.

And from this noble launching pad, Professor Grayling has embarked upon a two-decade quest to define the very attributes of the word *philosopher* for my generation: university chairs, societal fellowships, a trenchant volume or two each year, a pleasant abode or so in the country, good food and good wine—lots and lots of good food and good wine. Oh, do not get me wrong. It is not that Professor Grayling has been a renegade in this particular form of philosophical pursuit. Far from it—there are literally throngs and throngs just like him, all scratching out their subsistence in all the collegial wings. But in Professor Grayling we have the man who has established himself at the forefront of this ivory-towered brigade, primarily through the means of his considerable marketing talent. Not only has Professor Grayling proven remarkably adept in bringing his message to the masses, he has managed to bring the very essence of *himself* to the masses, thereby convincing a weekend breakfast audience that the trappings of a philosophy professor's life constitute the good life of modern perspicacity. From editorial boards to off-Broadway theater, Professor Grayling has rubbed a hair-bedraped shoulder against nearly every intelligentsia-favored artifact of this all-too-leisurely age, and the Sunday supplement public has eaten it up. Ask anyone in the know: Professor A. C. Grayling has gathered quite the following.

Well, of course he has gathered a *following*.

And the definiteness in crucial conception propping up this mass appeal? The brilliance of metaphor and poetical qualities tugging at the heartstrings of this admiring audience? Let us sift through Professor Grayling's dazzling arguments on the subject of death:

> "The fundamental question is how to deal with others' deaths. We grieve the loss of an element in what made our world meaningful. There is an unavoidable process of healing—of making whole—to be endured, marked in many societies by formal periods of mourning, between one and three years long. But the world is never again entire after bereavement. We do not get over losses; we merely learn to live with them.
>
> "There is a great consolation. Two facts—that the dead once lived; and that one loved them and mourned their loss—are inexpungeably part of the world's history. So the presence of those who lived can never be removed from time, which is to say that there is a kind of eternity after all."
> (Grayling 2003)

I admit freely to my bias: I do not belong to the Sunday Times intelligentsia, I am not one of those in the know and I am not a member of Professor Grayling's admiring crowd. For me this excerpt, along with all the rest, is pabulum I might forgive only coming from a pre-pubescent child—how am I to tolerate it off the pen of a man trumpeting his abilities to think for himself? Elsewhere in his remarks regarding Wittgenstein, Professor Grayling put forths that Wittgenstein holds the distinction of being the last of a breed—history's final example of a non-academically trained philosopher. I cannot say for certain whether this assertion of Professor Grayling's might indeed be true, but if it is, I would note it also marks the end of an entire era—the end of all that has been creative, useful and eye-opening in the realm of philosophical thought. Because there has never been, and there never will be, a true philosopher of the *academic* kind. When I consider the example of Wittgenstein and others much like him—such as Thoreau, Schopenhauer, Kierkegaard and Nietzsche—I recognize a truism at work that would be dangerous to overlook: a philosopher for the ages cannot possibly be the philosopher of his day. And, of course, vice versa.

Listen. I am just a simple man from Indiana. I cannot distinguish the good life from a good swig of beer. I have not the slightest idea what it takes to be a philosopher. But I do know exactly what it takes *not* to be a philosopher, and if I could just get Professor A. C. Grayling's pompous fat ass up on a pedestal, I could put it on display for everyone to see.

Oh, wait—he has already done it for me.

Fossilization

You cannot create literature as a professional writer. You cannot discover breakthrough knowledge as a professional scientist. You cannot inspire mankind as a professional philosopher.

When we take our most treasured enterprises and transform them into commodities, we destroy all their merit. We now have millions of writers, but no brilliant words. We now have millions of scientists, but no useful insight. We now have millions of philosophers, but no courageous wisdom.

Academia is fossilizing humanity's worth.

Apologia

Often what is needed is not new evidence, but a better home for the evidence one already has.

Reflections on the Work of Richard Klein

Richard G. Klein is a paleoanthropologist and currently a professor at Stanford University. His work and his writings have done much to provide evidence for and to popularize the out-of-Africa theory of human evolution (known more scientifically as the recent single-origin hypothesis). This theory postulates that *Homo sapiens*—who have been anatomically indistinguishable from modern humans since about 150 to 200 thousand years ago—experienced a sudden and decisive change in behavior beginning around 50 thousand years ago; and concurrent with this change, *Homo sapiens* undertook a major migratory expansion out of Africa, soon swamping and extincting the similarly lineaged populations *Homo neanderthalensis* and *Homo erectus*, eventually becoming the overwhelming biological force we now can witness all around this planet. Over the last two decades, this theory has been supported by a growing accumulation of archaeological and genetic evidence, so much so that the theory is now accepted almost universally, and unless and until new contradictory evidence comes to light, the out-of-Africa theory must be considered as the definitive framework for describing recent human evolution.

Richard Klein seems to be a rare beast among modern scientists. He is plain spoken, more attracted to evidence and theory than to academic politics, and—note this especially—he tackles large scientific questions, not the mere trivialities that pad most curriculum vitae. In fact, the central question of Klein's work—what were the circumstances that prompted man to cross that great conceptual divide from simple primate to complex cultural being—stands as perhaps the most important unanswered question currently facing modern science. And if anyone has made more progress in shining a clarifying light on that question than Richard Klein has, I have yet to see it.

Much of Klein's summarization of human evolution can be found inside his two books *The Human Career: Human Biological and Cultural Origins* (Klein 2009) and *The Dawn of Human Culture* (Klein 2002). However, for the purpose of the central question of Klein's work, there are two short and readily available presentations that encapsulate most of his essential ideas. The first is a lecture entitled *Behavioral and Biological Origins of Modern Humans* (Klein 1997), delivered to the California

Academy of Sciences in 1997. The second is a paper published in 2008, *Out of Africa and the Evolution of Human Behavior* (Klein 2008), which can be regarded as an update to the evidence presented in the earlier lecture with Klein's views still essentially intact. These two presentations are both excellent examples of scientific clarity and honesty (so much so that many academicians might have a hard time recognizing them as scientific), and I urge anyone not already familiar with Klein's ideas to devote an hour or so to reading through these two documents—it will be time well invested on what is a fundamental and extremely important topic.

Although there are several scientists who have contributed to our understanding of the out-of-Africa theory, the area where Klein has most distinguished himself is in the painting of a clear, evidence-backed portrait of how *sudden* the *Homo sapiens* transformation was beginning around 50 thousand years ago and how *overwhelming* was its impact and expansive reach. Pointing to the fossil and archaeological evidence, Klein describes three distinct *Homo*-based populations that existed just prior to 50 thousand years ago: 1. the remnant lineage from *Homo erectus*, the successors from an earlier (over 1 million years ago) exodus from Africa, living primarily in the habitable areas of Asia; 2. *Homo neanderthalensis*, a branch that had been occupying parts of Europe and the Middle East since around 400 thousand years ago; and 3. *Homo sapiens*, still in Africa and evolved into the anatomical form of modern humans by around 150 to 200 thousand years ago.

Although these three populations were geographically distinct and possessed distinguishing anatomical features, they were also remarkably alike in many fundamental respects. For one, they all had similar brain size, and perhaps more importantly, they all had similar behavior— behavior that could be captured in a single word … unremarkable.

Klein takes great pains to demonstrate that in site after site dating prior to 50 thousand years ago, there is no evidence to be found of form-based tools, artwork, jewelry, clothing, weaponry, etc., artifacts that soon will be making a sudden and explosive appearance on the human stage. He underscores that although *Homo*-based populations had certainly undergone behavioral changes since branching off from the other primates some seven million years earlier, the behaviors prior to just 50 thousand years ago were still far more comparable to older primate behaviors than to the modern behaviors that were about to emerge. Indeed, one can surmise that if an alien intelligence had visited this planet just prior to 50 thousand years ago, it would have found nothing remarkable about *any* of these *Homo*-based populations—these were simply primates scratching out their subsistence, indistinguishable bit players in the immense Earthly chorus of survival and procreation. Considering their meager numbers, and looking dispassionately at the fossil and archaeological evidence that Klein presents to us, we would have to conclude there was nothing in the circumstances of these *Homo*-based populations that would mark them as anything more than animal.

And then suddenly everything changed. And it has not stopped changing since.

The astonishing alteration first appeared near East Africa, right around 50 thousand years ago. In that location—and quickly expanding from there—you suddenly could find ostrich shell beads, form-based tools such as needles and awls, evidence of fishing technology, female figurines, clothing, burial displays, weapons galore. These suddenly innovative *Homo sapiens* soon began reaching into Europe and Asia, leaving behind a trail of newfound abilities literally everywhere along the path. They quickly overwhelmed and extincted the Neanderthals (Klein passionately describes the profound effect it had on him to see the sophisticated remnants of Cro-magnon culture (*Homo sapiens*) layered right on top of the less sophisticated artifacts of the Neanderthals, evidence of no intervening gap), and although the archaeological record is less complete in Asia, in part due to the ongoing interference of modern governments, it would appear *Homo erectus* also suffered a similar fate at the hands of these rapidly moving invaders. Their new mastery allowed *Homo sapiens* to boat to Australia by as early as 40 thousand years ago. Their unprecedented trapping, textile and construction techniques enabled them to inhabit colder climates, including Siberia, thus leading the way across the then dry Bering Strait and straight into the Americas. By ten thousand years ago, humanity had become so technologically adept it could begin trading its hunter-gatherer existence for domesticated animals and crops, and by six thousand years ago the species was building enormous civilizations and recording for posterity its burgeoning feats. By five hundred years ago, man could … well, you already know what man could do by then—just take a good look around.

It is hard to say which has been the more impressive: the *suddenness* of man's transformation, or the *power* of his planet-conquering reach. One thing is for certain: compared to the accomplishments of the previous 50 thousand years (or the previous 5 million years for that matter), these post-transformation exploits of *Homo sapiens* can only be described as stunning—stunning to an infinite degree.

But you need not take my word for it. Richard Klein has already laid out this entire tableau in exquisite detail, and he has seen all the evidence first hand.

As certain and insistent as Klein sounds about the immediacy and effectiveness of the *Homo sapiens* revolution, he sounds equally *uncertain* about the reasons why.

Klein has put forth—quite tentatively, I might add—what he describes as the most "economic" explanation for man's great leap forward, positing a sudden genetic mutation, one powerful enough to produce significant and immediate neurological impact, such as the kind that would induce rapidly spoken language. Against this thesis, it is commonly asserted within the academic community that the buildup to the *Homo sapiens* transformation must have been far more gradual than that, with various kinds of social and cultural evolutionary change— such as additional reliance on the nuclear family, an altered diet, theory of mind acquisition, a budding adaptability to change—all serving as the necessary forerunners to the dramatic upshot still to come.

Klein easily and quite rightly dismisses such counter proposals. In the first place, these explanations would need to be counted as tautological at best, since they are essentially positing that *Homo sapiens'* behavior changed because *Homo sapiens'* behavior changed. But even disregarding that obvious logical weakness, Klein demonstrates with the stubborn insistence of cold hard facts that such explanations are completely at odds with the fossil and archaeological record. Any slow evolutionary accretion of dramatically unique cultural and social conduct—including behaviors that would have been dependent upon a sophisticated use of language—could not have conceivably taken place without leaving behind a conspicuous trail of evidence. But what little (and mostly questionable) evidence has been offered in support of these evolutionary precursors ends up looking paltry and sparse next to the abundantly rich artifacts associated with the post-transformation epoch. Klein recognizes such vague explanations as not based upon the preponderance of evidence but instead as the type of fuzzy, non-committal solution generally favored by academicians—academicians who cannot be bothered by either logic or facts.

Klein is a scientist who *insists* on being bothered by logic and facts, which is why I suspect he is being so hesitant—for *his* explanation has myriad problems of its own.

The challenge of uncovering the catalyst behind *Homo sapiens'* sudden transformation must seem like a type of lock to Klein, one for which he has gauged its characteristics with a painstaking accuracy. He knows the contours of the many tumblers, has measured the keyhole for size, understands all too well the quick-releasing mechanism. He can dismiss the vague academic solutions as scarcely qualifying for keys at all—perhaps more than anyone else he can recognize the need here for something more tangible and immediate. Yet economically speaking, how many reasonable solutions actually exist? After all, Klein seems to be wanting to convince us—and to convince himself—is there not only one? A genetic mutation holds the promise of suddenness; a significantly altered neurological structure carries the potential for effective power. But in appealing to the genome and human brain for explaining mankind's astonishing transformation, Klein falls victim to that same fatal illness now plaguing the entirety of modern science—he has infused both genetics and neurology with an implausible human magic.

Intelligence, language, memory, numeracy, artistry, technological tool-producing vision—the scientific literature is now chock-full of genetic and neurological descriptions accounting for this entire host of impressive cognitive and behavioral skills. In genetic paper after genetic paper, you will find the microarray analysis protocols, the sequence-based samples, all lined up impressively along one side, and matched against that glorious detail you will find the list of unparalleled traits and attributes that have cast *Homo sapiens* as distinctively modern. *Voilà*, the genetic scientists all seem to say, and we break into terrific applause. But should an inquiring voice call out from the back of the room and wonder what connects transcription to observable behavior, what bit of mechanism links nucleotide to lyric poem, that voice will be greeted with an uncomfortably lengthy pause. Marvelous genetics here, astonishing behavior there, but in between ... not one single connecting step.

The human brain has fared no better. In neurological paper after neurological paper, you will find entire albums of fMRI photographs, brilliant diffusion tensor pictures, all plastered across their pages in a technicolor glory, and matched against that vivid detail you will find the list of unparalleled traits and attributes that have cast *Homo sapiens* as distinctively modern. *Voilà*, the cognitive scientists all seem to say, and we break into terrific applause. But should an inquiring voice call out from the back of the room and wonder what connects resonance image to actual behavior, what bit of mechanism links synapse to third root of pi, that voice will be greeted with an uncomfortably lengthy pause. Vibrant images here, rational behavior there, but in between ... not one single connecting step.

These connecting steps are not some mere trivial detail, not the mop-up work for a graduate student assistant; and yet even those scientists who can appreciate the importance of such linkages will speak as though their discovery is simply a matter of time. The secrets of human genetics and human neurology *must* emerge, these scientists all seem a little too willing to assure us, because in fact the scientific community has already *accepted* genetics and neurology as the driving force behind mankind's cognitive and behavioral splendor—no demonstration is apparently required.

But that state of affairs must seem a bit awkward for Richard Klein, whose mutation hypothesis, perhaps more than anything else, needs precisely that demonstration. Because without it, Klein's hypothesis does not even rise to the level of relevance.

Intelligence, language, memory, numeracy, artistry, technological tool-producing vision—the scope and potency of that list can only be regarded as downright shocking, for there is no evidence *any* of these skills existed prior to 50 thousand years ago. The scene Klein lays before us is extraordinarily surprising, nothing at all like what might have been predicted. Its timeline defies every temporal characteristic of evolutionary history, its details contradict all expectation of species. So unique is the story of the *Homo sapiens* transformation that it might be more prudent to think evolution and biology must have played no role at all. In any *typical* approach to animal domains and behavior, genetic mutations would be expected to do their work only gradually, stepwise upon the species—their transmittal spread out across many generations, if not across entire ages. In any *typical* approach to animal domains and behavior, neurological restructurings would be expected to produce their impact only locally, specific to particular function—not fostering a cognitive reformulation extending from ear to ear.

But there is economy to consider after all, along with the confident assurances from modern science, and so rather than pursuing any *unusual* solutions to this preeminently unusual story, what could be more pragmatic than to turn to the *typical* approaches, and just give them a little anthropocentric boost.

In many respects, Klein's mutation hypothesis and modern science's genetic-neurological certainty are now the ideal soul mates, the perfectly matched couple. Klein's hypothesis receives from the promises of genetic and neurological science all the cognitive and behavioral power that his theory so desperately needs, while in turn, modern science gets from Klein's extraordinary anthropological story all the permission it could possibly want in order to study *human* genetics and neurology with an entirely different approach, with the license, with the justification—no, with the *requirement*—to ignore and break all the typical biological rules.

But tell me this: with each of these constructs leaning so heavily against the other, and resting apparently upon nothing else, why have we become so certain that they cannot collectively fall?

I think in some sense Richard Klein must already know all this, must feel the reasonable doubt somewhere deep within his tentative bones. I can admire his adamant courage, the plain-spoken insistence that the *Homo sapiens* transformational lock must have been opened only by a specific and tangible key, and I can understand his pragmatic desire to turn to the common and widely accepted mechanisms, resting comfortably on the assurances of modern science. But even Richard Klein must realize—must realize somewhere deep within his tentative bones—that in casting human genetics and the human brain into the role of *Homo sapiens'* transformational unlocking key, he must first bend and twist genetics and neurology all out of any recognizable, usable, or plausible shape.

An economic explanation—or should I say a scientifically *magical* explanation—is not worthy of Klein's extraordinary story.

So where does that leave us?

In recent years, I have been making the suggestion that there is an alternative way of looking at Klein's tableau, as well as looking at almost every facet of human behavior associated with it. I have become convinced that Klein's unusual anthropological story has in fact an unusual anthropological solution, a solution that defines—no, actually *is*—human atypicality. This solution is of course nothing like the cultural evolutionary theories favored by the vague academicians, and it is also nothing like the sudden genetic/neurological mutation hypothesized by Richard Klein. In the context of the entire out-of-Africa discussion, it must seem like an idea that comes from straight out of the blue, if not from straight out of nah-nah land. I understand all that, but must insist on making my suggestion all the same, because nearly everything in Richard Klein's peerless anthropological work points invariably in its direction.

My suggestion of course is autism. Autism is the key that fits that lock.

If we are going to understand the role autism must have played in man's great leap forward (and continues to play in man's ongoing transformation today), it becomes necessary first to see autism for what it truly is, a task made nearly impossible in recent years due to the debilitating grip of modern science. Modern science has already made its pronouncement upon autism, despite not knowing yet exactly what autism is—but never mind that, because the pronouncement has been made and the pronouncement is exceedingly grim. Autism is an illness. Autism is a developmental disaster. Autism is the incomparable tragedy of parents, the unspeakable burden of all mankind. If you listen carefully enough, you will hear inside that pronouncement an unflinching confidence and assurance—it is a confidence and assurance we have already encountered.

In a reversal of ironic proportions, that same collective mindset that has already *accepted* genetics and neurology as the undoubted catalyst behind all modern human behavior, now becomes the collective mindset demanding of autism that it be the foremost example of genetics and neurology gone bad. In autism study after autism study, you will find the fragmented copy number variants, the brittle axon-fiber connections, all lined up lugubriously along one side, and matched against that woeful detail you will find the list of traits and attributes that have cast autistic individuals as purportedly broken. *Voilà*, the autism scientists all seem to say, and we break into a respectful applause. But should an inquiring voice call out from the back of the room and wonder what connects fractured genome to unusual behavior, what bit of mechanism links fraying neuron to rhythmically flapping hand, that voice will be greeted with an uncomfortably lengthy pause. Research findings here, atypical individuals there, but in between ... not one single connecting step.

The failure to supply these steps was, in the case of human intelligence, language, artistry and the like, an unfortunate circumstance, because along with the unjustified assurance that such steps would soon be found, it has prevented scientists from considering an alternative course. But in the case of autism, this same failure to supply these connecting steps, along with the undemonstrated certainty that autistic individuals are medically doomed—this practice has become the foremost example of unbridled cruelty. This practice denounces, without the first shred of understanding, nearly one percent of the human population as waste— the large majority of whom must be working quietly and productively among us. This practice denounces, without the first effort towards acceptance, nearly the entire autistic population as pariah—when that population might be better described as mankind's deliverance. Modern science's confident assurance regarding autism is in fact a massive instance of scientific blindness, one that has rendered nearly the entire human population utterly oblivious to who autistic individuals actually are, and utterly oblivious to what they have amazingly done.

Autism can be accurately depicted without resorting to science's insistence on genetic disorder and neurological disease—without resorting to any cruelty. The key concepts are species, recognition and perception. Autism's fundamental description goes essentially like this: autistic individuals, to a significant degree, do not readily recognize or attach to the human species, and thus cannot easily organize their experiences or perceptions around that species and its members (as is the case for non-autistic individuals). In consequence, autistic individuals organize their sensory world instead by an entirely different form of perception, a perception engaged primarily by the symmetry, structure and pattern that inherently stands out from the surrounding, non-biological world.

It is that different form of perception—the *autistic* form of perception—that has launched *Homo sapiens* off the East African plains and straight into the modern world.

The *Homo*-based circumstances Klein describes from prior to 50 thousand years ago are circumstances typical of nearly every animal species. Prior to man's great leap forward, the human cognitive focus would have been directed towards survival and procreation alone, and human perceptual recognition and attachment would have been centered upon the species itself, exclusively upon its own members and behaviors. This intense species recognition and attachment is an evolutionary trait that must run deeply throughout the entire animal kingdom—biologists can see evidence of it nearly everywhere—and this trait of course has been critically important in helping hold species together, keeping their members gathered near sources of shelter, food and sex. The perceptual characteristics behind an intense intra-species focus help account for the behaviors of the genus *Homo* over many millions of years, and the same perceptual characteristics help explain also the behaviors of the species *Homo sapiens* for the largest portion of its existence. Intense species recognition and attachment is the primary reason that for a substantially long period of time—right up to 50 thousand years ago—man remained behaviorally indistinguishable from the rest of the animal world.

This intense species recognition and attachment has not disappeared from the human species—not in the slightest. Despite mankind having now undertaken a complete overhaul to its environmental circumstances, an overhaul of nearly breathtaking proportions, and despite humanity having reassembled nearly all its former survival and procreative needs into a more distinctively modern garb, still, for the vast majority of the human population, its primary perceptual focus continues to be directed to all the old familiar targets—food, power, politics, safety, sex. Man still gathers gregariously around what he perceives of as popular; man continues to take his foremost comfort in the presence of others. When you examine carefully the preferred behaviors of nearly every *typical* human being (non-autistic human beings), you will quickly realize that man has not abandoned in the slightest his intense focus on his own species, has not shed one bit the innate ability to recognize and attach to other humans. For a large percentage of the human population, these species-focused perceptions have been carried forward essentially intact, right into modern times.

Furthermore, this intense species recognition and attachment has not been without value in advancing the human cultural transformation. A key component behind both the widespread nature and the swiftness of human behavioral and environmental change is that most humans continue to be profusely imitative of their own kind. This replicative effect is ubiquitous, but is most critical during the developmental years of children, guaranteeing that each new generation will readily adopt the current circumstances of species—no matter what those circumstances might happen to be. When humans were once hunter-gatherers, their children became hunter-gatherers too. When humans began building civilizations, their children joined right in without skipping a beat. When adults spoke Latin, their children spoke Latin as well, and when adults moved on to modern Italian, their children fell right into imitative line. Just as it once held the human species together for strictly survival and procreative purposes, this trait of intense species recognition and attachment now holds humanity together while it cascades forward through an accelerating, mostly non-biological revolution.

And yet as powerful as these strong species-specific perceptions can be in keeping a species assembled, this trait is also extraordinarily conservative with respect to a species' current circumstances—no matter what those circumstances might happen to be. The evidence of this conservatism is abundant, it can be found in the static circumstances of nearly every animal species. The effect of this conservatism hits extremely close to home, for it cemented the static circumstances of the genus *Homo* over many millions of years. To catalyze sudden and enormous behavioral change would require a crack to appear in this intense intra-species recognition and attachment, would require that a species be able to perceive beyond just survival and procreation, beyond just itself. But if we take into account the ongoing, long-lasting, extremely static circumstances of nearly every animal species—every animal species, that is, except for modern man—we would have to conclude any alternative form of perception not strongly focused upon the species itself would have to be a form of perception exceedingly rare, would have to be a form of perception that, biologically speaking, could only be described as exceptionally atypical.

If autism is, at its root, a significant inability to recognize and attach to other members of the species, as well as to their extant behaviors and conditions, then autism already carries within itself all the difficulties frequently reported for autistic individuals—that is, any of their so-called disabilities are circumstantially earned, they do not need the superfluous addendum of a medical cause. Development in *typical* individuals is heavily influenced by species attachment and imitation, and therefore any corresponding development in autistic individuals is bound to be slow, frustrating and at odds with all the rest. Social adeptness in the *non-autistic* population is simply the natural result of the common recognitions and attachments within the species, and thus it is not at all surprising that autistic individuals, lacking these common recognitions and attachments, are viewed to exist in a world apart, are judged to be socially disconnected. In fact, the real mystery regarding autism is that it ever managed to take hold within the human population at all, given that its fundamental characteristic runs so counter to a basic support of survival and procreation. But take hold autism has; and thus it would not be unreasonable to ask of scientists that they pause for a moment and contemplate the consequence.

Without a strong species recognition and attachment to help organize their experiences and perceptions, autistic individuals, especially *young* autistic individuals, are faced with the daunting task of overcoming a nearly complete sensory chaos. Typical individuals organize their experiences around other people; typical individuals organize their perceptions around what other people do. But autistic individuals, significantly detached from the other members of the population, cannot organize their sensory experiences in quite the same way (with a variety of sensory difficulties naturally resulting). Fortunately for autistic individuals, and fortunately for the entire human race, the non-biological world seems to have supplied an *alternative* form of perceptual organization, one that has remained apparently untapped right up until around 50 thousand years ago.

It would be difficult to describe at its most fundamental level the nature of these self-organizing environmental features, or to explain what it is about them that causes them to *inherently* stand out. But for the purposes of this discussion it is enough to note that humans have recognized and distinguished these organizing features through the use of such names as symmetry, repetition, mapping, pattern, structure and form. From the sensory chaos that would otherwise be their fate, autistic individuals, especially *young* autistic individuals, focus on and organize their sensory experiences around these surrounding, mostly non-biological elements of symmetry, structure and pattern. This becomes most evident when observing the characteristic autistic behaviors, often called restricted or repetitive behaviors—lining up toys, spinning wheels, turning on and off switches, rhythmically flapping hands—behaviors abundantly steeped in pattern, behaviors profusely intent on form. Although the autistic perceptual focus will often broaden with age, even to the point of eventually incorporating species and social interests, when we examine carefully the preferred behaviors of nearly every *atypical* human being (autistic human beings), we will quickly realize that instead of organizing their experiences around other people and around the species itself, autistic individuals gravitate more frequently to those perceptions organized around the various structures that naturally emerge from the surrounding, non-biological world.

And it is not just in the preferred behaviors of autistic individuals that we can witness the influence of these non-biological, self-organizing concepts. Intelligence, language, memory, numeracy, artistry, technological tool-producing vision—at the core of each behavioral element on that list, at the core of each behavioral element marking the sudden human transformation, you will find a deep foundational reliance upon these very same concepts, the concepts of symmetry, repetition, mapping, pattern, structure, form. Autistic individuals, through the needful circumstances of their rather precarious biological condition, have opened a perspective onto a world that goes far beyond immediate biological need, goes far beyond the tightly gripping focus of survival and procreation alone. And by bringing their unique perspective to *Homo sapiens* itself, autistic individuals have spawned an unprecedented biological revolution—they have jarred the human species entirely from its former animal course.

Much like Klein's mutation hypothesis, my suggestion regarding autism is a theory not easily falsifiable, not if falsifiability requires measuring the autistic presence and influence of 50 thousand years ago. For the moment, we must remain content with weighing evidence that is more indirect, such as those studies demonstrating that non-autistic children are more naturally drawn to human-derived biological images, while autistic children are more attracted to non-biological contingencies possessing pattern and form (Klin et al. 2009). But perhaps an even more compelling reason for considering autism as the likely catalyst behind man's great leap forward is to recognize that autism-inspired behavioral and environmental change continues apace all around us, even at an accelerating rate. The great leap forward did not come to an end on the East African plains, it was not just a solitary event from 50 thousand years ago. That same transforming phenomenon exists right before our very eyes, we can witness its ongoing impact nearly each and every day.

To take just one instance from many—a prominent instance—we can consider the case of Isaac Newton and his inspired laws, along with the resulting industrial, scientific revolution. Here we find a single individual—an individual known for his unusual demeanor, an individual known for being socially detached—filled suddenly with a strange new perspective upon his surrounding, mostly non-biological world, drawn deeply into the patterns and structures no human had ever perceived before. By reconstructing the form of his unique vision through the use of such tools as language and mathematics—tools which themselves are richly steeped in form and pattern, tools which themselves were greatly augmented by Newton's innovative perception—by reconstructing the form of his vision into the human environment itself, Newton made his surprising perceptions accessible to nearly all. From there, humanity's gregarious, imitative, self-preserving nature took care of the matter of dissemination, and in less than two hundred years time man's cognitive, behavioral and material world had become entirely transformed. The unusual perceptions of one atypical man, followed swiftly by an overwhelming human revolution—it is a narrative that by now should sound remarkably familiar.

The discoveries of Newton's laws of motion, gravitation and optics were obviously not the result of a genetic mutation; the resulting industrial, scientific revolution was clearly not brought about by a universal synaptic rewiring (although I certainly would not put it past modern scientists to attempt those foolish claims). The only plausible, sufficiently pliant location for human intelligence, language, artistry and the like is the human environment itself. Only there can the features of human revolutionary change be creatively introduced, innovatively modified, by individuals with an unusually broadened eye. Only there can these same features be imitatively multiplied, spread rapidly from place to place, by a species focused on one another, by a species focused on enhancing its self-preserving interests. In this mechanism we see the elements of both *suddenness* and *power*, we see the two essential ingredients at the heart of Klein's out-of-Africa story.

If you search the Internet you can find a web site devoted to something called the *Neanderthal theory of autism*—what appears to be a very loose mixture of dubious anthropology alongside vague suggestions that autism reflects distinctive Neanderthal behaviors passed along through interbred human genes. I will let the dubious anthropology speak for itself, but as for the notion there were any distinctive Neanderthal behaviors that could have been passed along in any particular way, Klein's paleoanthropology sounds the death knell to all of that. Nowhere in the fossil or archaeological record can there be found the slightest indication that Neanderthals behaved in ways differently than primitive primates; Neanderthals exhibited an unremarkable lifestyle that continued unabated right up to the point of their extinction. The

Neanderthals were *overrun* by the human big bang; they were not its participants.

There is one aspect to this notion, however, that has potentially productive merit. Recent genetic analysis (Green et al. 2010; very preliminary, still subject to verification) indicates there may be a small amount of Neanderthal-derived DNA currently within the human genome, with a strong indication this resulted from species intermixture that occurred *prior* to the *Homo sapiens* revolution. Such intermixture would not be entirely surprising; the different *Homo*-based populations shared fluid geographical boundaries, and interactions between Neanderthals and *Homo sapiens* could have taken place on numerous occasions, with gene flow possible in either or both directions. If so, such an intermingling of genetic material could provide a conceivable mechanism for explaining the characteristics of a species non-recognition. That is, it could be surmised that beyond a certain threshold, the presence of intermixed species genes might produce in certain individuals a difficulty in recognizing and attaching to the other members of the population around them—precisely the characteristic described above as the fundamental basis of autism.

All this would be highly speculative of course, with a good deal still to be explained, and the most that could be suggested for now is that as genetic information continues to be gathered from autistic individuals, Neanderthal fossils, and the entire human species, a comparative analysis is possibly warranted. It should be noted, however, that even if it were true that moderate species intermixture provides a mechanism for a species non-recognition, that explanation would only give rise to a still larger and perhaps more difficult question, since such a mechanism would not be uniquely human. Over Earth's vast history we would expect to see thousands, if not millions, of similar inter-species events; but as far as we know, it has been only in *Homo sapiens* that autism has taken hold. Autism's intrinsic survival and procreative disadvantages do provide some expectation that autism would only *rarely* gain species traction; but still, it must be answered why the outcome was entirely different some 50 thousand years ago. What was it that uniquely turned that particular moment into such a stunningly explosive event?

Through his stubborn insistence on appealing to the evidence of the archaeological and fossil record, and through his stubborn insistence in arguing for both the suddenness and the power of mankind's remarkable turn, Richard Klein has presented humanity with an exquisite challenge—the challenge of explaining the species' own shocking history. Klein's proposal for how that unprecedented transformation might have come to be—a sudden and rare genetic mutation producing significant neurological effect—it remains true to the parameters of Klein's presentation, but falls victim to the anthropocentric failings of modern science.

Klein's anthropological work has been far too extraordinary, far too clarifying, to be cast as victim; Klein's exquisite challenge deserves an equally exquisite solution. Thus it is that I suggest autism as the key to the out-of-Africa story. Autism—quirky, fragile, misunderstood, too often cruelly treated—autism represents that form of human perception not focused upon the species itself but instead upon the symmetry, pattern and structure to be found in the surrounding, non-biological world. It is that atypical form of perception that has driven humanity's atypical turn, and it is that atypical form of perception that continues to catalyze human change right through the present day.

The Purpose-Driven Life

Although not as often now as when I was young,
It still happens upon this planet's burning surface
A child will spot a model on the toy store shelf
And turn instantly beguiled.
Space shuttle, Eiffel Tower, late-model car,
Three-masted ship—it matters not,
The glossy image on the box beckons
With hue, decal and precision.
The child is cast as a willing slave,
A slave to construction's glory.

Perhaps blessed with parents possessing eyes
For budding wonderment, perhaps
Resourceful enough to tug on a reluctant sleeve,
Our child gets his wish fulfilled,
And on the ride home even the road squirms
With anticipation: piece fitting cleanly to piece,
Red enamel coating with audacious warmth,
The finished product speeding at speeds,
Scaling at heights heretofore unknown
Inside playroom walls.

With shrink-wrap ripped and flaps torn to reveal contents,
His enthusiasm might still be rising …
But the pieces indeed are many.
Glue. There is never enough glue,
And then there is way too much glue.
Instructions first set aside as slighting insults
Now mock as hieroglyph from the bedroom floor.
Nothing fits to fit, paint smears and never where intended to smear,
And Dad is none too happy about what has happened to the rug.
One day, perhaps two days, certainly no more than a week,
His hollow feelings unrelieved this child begins to wonder
If the dream was worth a dream. The tragedy is,

He does not yet know the depths of his own despair,
For this is after all only a model, with a scale of one to infinity.

The purpose-driven life overwhelms us with detail and size,
Each goal seemingly checked by circumstance,
All steps unveiling a wider vision of the massive structure
Yet to build. Pieces fill a range from quark to cosmos,
Construction lasts from bang to farthest light-year reach.
How to comfort a child with lessons of effort and patience
When we stand so dumbstruck and numb ourselves?
The ancients always warned us, God is surely boundless—
Now we know, they were not kidding.

Bibliography

(Baron-Cohen et al. 2007): Baron-Cohen, Simon; Robinson, Janine; Woodbury-Smith, Marc; Wheelwright, Sally. 2007. "Very Late Diagnosis of Asperger Syndrome: The Cambridge Lifespan Asperger Syndrome Service (CLASS)." Interactive Autism Network. http://www.iancommunity.org/cs/articles/very_late_diagnosis_of_asperger_syndrome.

(Boyer 1968): Boyer, Carl B. 1968. *A History of Mathematics*. New York: Wiley.

(Chomsky 1957): Chomsky, Noam. 1957. *Syntactic Structures*. The Hague: Mouton.

(Chomsky 1965): Chomsky, Noam. 1965. *Aspects of the Theory of Syntax*. Cambridge: MIT Press.

(Dawson et al. 2007): Dawson, Michelle; Soulières, Isabelle; Gernsbacher, Morton Ann; Mottron, Laurent. 2007. "The Level and Nature of Autistic Intelligence." *Psychological Science* 18:657–62.

(Dembski 2008): Dembski, William (July 11, 2008). "FIRST-PERSON: Faith & Healing—Where's the Evidence?" Baptist Press. http://www.bpnews.net/BPnews.asp?ID=28460.

(Flynn 2007): Flynn, James R. 2007. *What Is Intelligence?: Beyond the Flynn Effect*. Cambridge: Cambridge University Press.

(Ganz 2006): Ganz, Michael. 2006. "The Costs of Autism." *Understanding Autism: From Basic Neuroscience to Treatment*. Editors Moldin and Rubenstein. Boca Raton: Taylor & Francis.

(Goldacre 2008): Goldacre, Ben. 2008. *Bad Science.* London: Fourth Estate.

(Grayling 1988): Grayling, A. C. 1988. *Wittgenstein.* Oxford: Oxford University Press.

(Grayling 2003): Grayling, A. C. 2003. *Meditations for the Humanist: Ethics for a Secular Age.* Oxford: Oxford University Press.

(Green et al. 2010): Green, Richard E. and many others. 2010. "A Draft Sequence of the Neandertal Genome." *Science* 328:710–22.

(Kierkegaard, *Practice in Christianity*): Kierkegaard, Soren. *Practice in Christianity.* Translation by H.V. Hong and E.H. Hong. 1991. Princeton: Princeton University Press. (Text slightly altered.)

(Klein 1997): Klein, Richard G. 1997. "Behavioral and Biological Origins of Modern Humans." Access Excellence. http://www.accessexcellence.org/BF/bf02/klein/index.php.

(Klein 2002): Klein, Richard G. 2002. *The Dawn of Human Culture.* New York: Wiley.

(Klein 2008): Klein, Richard G. 2008. "Out of Africa and the Evolution of Human Behavior." *Evolutionary Anthropology* 17: 267–81.

(Klein 2009): Klein, Richard G. 2009. *The Human Career: Human Biological and Cultural Origins, 3rd Edition.* Chicago: University of Chicago Press.

(Klin et al. 2009): Klin, Ami; Lin, David J.; Gorrindo, Phillip; Ramsay, Gordon; Jones, Warren. 2009. "Two-year-olds with Autism Orient to Non-Social Contingencies Rather than Biological Motion." *Nature* 459: 257–61.

(Pinker 1994): Pinker, Steven. 1994. *The Language Instinct: How the Mind Creates Language.* New York: Morrow.

(Pinker 2002): Pinker, Steven. 2002. *The Blank Slate: The Modern Denial of Human Nature.* New York: Viking.